A Unique Generation: 70+

Living "it up" in a retirement community

Renate Donovan and Patricia Haensly

Illustrations
By
Shirley Walters

authorHOUSE®

AuthorHouse™
1663 Liberty Drive
Bloomington, IN 47403
www.authorhouse.com
Phone: 1-800-839-8640

First published by AuthorHouse 6/20/2011

ISBN: 978-1-4634-0187-0 (e)
ISBN: 978-1-4634-0188-7 (hc)
ISBN: 978-1-4634-0189-4 (sc)

Library of Congress Control Number: 2011908030

Printed in the United States of America

To

Our Families

Acknowledgments

We want to thank the many individuals who allowed us to write about their activities, as we described life in a particular retirement community. Their comments have given us the spirit and encouragement to complete the work. We especially want to thank John Fraser, Betsy Gilboy, Helen Hill, Marilyn Ivins, Esther Parks, and Jim Seamans, all residents of our "campus," for contributing their words and ideas to lend that personal touch. We are very grateful to Shirley Walters, whose vibrant illustrations embellish our text.

We are also grateful to Margot Curtis, who spent a great deal of time editing this volume, and Julia Cox, Patti Lozano, and Mary O'Connor, who gave freely of their expertise and many hours to help us with the technical aspect of this volume. Without them, we never could have finished. God bless all of you.

Both of us, your authors, in our early eighties, as well as our artist, are an integral part of this "unique" generation. We considered it our mission and a challenge to tell our story.

Renate Donovan and Patricia Haensly

Table of Contents

Prologue

Why are we writing this book? It's an odd story. The two of us live in a retirement community. We've been here between 4 and 5 years and we're having the time of our lives. We happened to meet near our mailboxes and one of us dropped a letter. As I bent over to retrieve the mail, I commented to the others jokingly "ah, the highlight of our day!" Each of us chuckled, but then we thought about our reaction, and both of us agreed that this is one of our daily chores, though definitely not the highlight of the day. We are intelligent women, up in years, yes, but full of hopes, dreams and plans for the future. We thought about this some more and realized that many of our acquaintances and family members, and even people in their sixties, see us as "passé," more than past our prime.

When we thought about the nature and purpose of life at age 70 and beyond, we were influenced in part by *The Third Chapter: Passion, Risk, and Adventure in the 25 years after 50* (Sarah Lawrence-Lightfoot. Sarah Crichton Books, Farrar, Straus and Giroux, New York. 2009). It came to our minds that we indeed were considering a fourth chapter of life, a time of life that could be just as full of passion, risk, and adventure, if we chose to shape it with that in mind. We decided that the purpose of this book would be to change the mindset of people about the purpose and possibilities of this period of life. Many of us who are 70 and above feel that we have value, and that our lives are meaningful to us and those around us. We are the new unique generation that hardly existed in past centuries. Whether it's improved medicine, living conditions or whatever, we are living longer. Our life has meaning and we can add a spark to the life of those around us, and of the younger generation coming along. With this in mind, we will occasionally refer to our "fourth chapter" of life.

Until recently, we were recognized when –

- Everyone we meet becomes very solicitous – not a bad thing
- Our grandchildren, now grown, offer to lug our carry-on when we travel
- Bran, prunes and Metamucil® become the important traditional meal of the day
- Our clothes get too long as we realize we are shrinking (men and women)
- Our memory becomes even shorter
- Our greatest enjoyment each day is our afternoon nap (for some)
- We listen patiently as our friends describe their illnesses in detail
- Our family doesn't trust our driving, and maybe they are right

- We don't hear as well as we used to, but we hate our hearing aids
- We actually enjoy being helped now, even though we take pride in our independence
- Pets become our favorite buddies
- We don't understand today's music
- We don't understand our grandkids' language
- We tire more easily
- When we travel, we worry more about carrying our medications than what we are going to wear on the trip
- The texture of toilet tissues becomes a major concern
- Our social calendar consists mainly of visits to doctors

This is just a brief list of what others think of us. With this book, we plan to change this erroneous perception. It may be true for some of us, but for most of us, life is a new adventure, a time to relish new friendships and new learning.

We invite the reader to follow along as we explore new opportunities, new options, and new ways to live successfully in our new home, a retirement community. This does not mean assisted living or a nursing home, but rather it means a "campus" for the unique generation, the super-seniors, in their 70's and beyond.

1

Why a Retirement Community?

As we started to write this book, we thought of including everyone, those of us who are in our 70's and beyond. But the numbers are tremendous, too big for the scope of this book. The authors have chosen this life style and we think it will interest our readers, especially those who don't know what to expect. This includes fear of leaving our homes, fear of the unknown, fear of how we'll fit in, and just being afraid of change. Moving to a retirement community can be a difficult decision. Many will never make this choice. However, it can be the beginning of something big. It can change your life, give you a new reason for living, a challenge for the future.

We have talked to a number of members of the "unique generation," who have decided to become part of a particular retirement community. We have also discussed how each of us arrived at this decision. We call ourselves "super-seniors." Come with us as we tell our stories, so that you can learn more about us. You might find some surprises.

Betsy is an attractive, perky 75-year old widow. Her view reflects the way many of us look at life in a retirement community. Please note, we do not call our new living arrangement a "retirement home." We are a community, a neighborhood of citizens in their 70's and beyond. Here is Betsy:

"I have just passed my 75th birthday and have moved into a retirement community. Why did I come here? To be near my children? Yes! To place myself in an environment with less responsibility and less pressure, where I could relax and be at peace for the rest of my days? Yes! But, much to my surprise, I found LIFE!!"

The wonderful seniors, 70 and up, up, up, are so alive – they are looking forward to their future. Now there is time to learn new things, experience excitement, have fun, travel, find new friendship and, yes, love.

"Since moving here I have learned to bowl wii® – am, in fact, captain of my bowling team. Also, I won a gold medal in the Area Senior Olympics for Washer Pitching.

"I entertain my new-found friends and neighbors more now than I ever did in the past. Of course, many of us get together in the morning over coffee to solve the

2

world's problems. After all, with all of our experience, we are certainly qualified.

"Since I've been here I danced for the first time in nine years, and, no, I had not forgotten how. I just haven't thought about dancing in a long time. What fun it is!

"I am continuing to grow. Not only from learning through shared experiences, but by attending seminars and workshops. I just bought a computer.

"Now I am focusing on staying alive (after all, I'm having a ball) by taking better care of myself through exercising my body and my mind.

"Seventy-five has become a new beginning for me. I leap out of bed in the morning (almost literally). I cannot wait to begin my day.

"My family appreciates my new-found happiness also. Now, when they talk about their adventures, I have interesting tales to tell. It's been a win, win for us all."

Other comments we have heard frequently from super-seniors emphasize the feeling of independence, freedom, and the ability to live life fully, perhaps for the first time in their adult years.

Shirley says: "I wanted to lift that burden from my children's shoulders. I wanted to make my own decision about where I would live the rest of my life. I did not want my daughter to have to find a suitable place for me when the time came to move. I found this wonderful community, I have new friends, I am never lonely. I can be alone when I want to be and I can have company when I feel like talking. I can play games, or bridge, or listen to music, or read a good book. It's all up to me."

2

A Day in the Life of a Super-Senior

How do we, super-seniors, spend a typical day? You might think we spend most of it on the telephone, contacting our loved ones, or perhaps resting and taking naps, as couch potatoes, watching television and some such restful non-activities. Far from it. Even our restful days are full of activities. Let us peek in on some of our fellow residents for a review of an ordinary day. The first one we'll visit is Helen. Helen is 85 years old and lives in a two-bedroom apartment on the first floor of a four-story building in her retirement community. She has a lovely patio that looks out on a large grassy ground with trees and a lake in the background. She rises daily at 6:00 a.m. Today is no exception. She fixes herself a cup of coffee and takes it out to the patio to admire the sunrise and watch some of the other early risers walk their dogs or just walk. Her husband, Keith, rises a little later. She takes time to putter in her small garden that surrounds the patio. Helen is very proud of her garden. She grows mostly shrubs and flowers, but also tends a tomato vine which is growing healthy fruit. She and Keith have placed a trellis on one side of the patio and have planted a butterfly vine to climb on the trellis. This gives them some privacy without obstructing the view. Although Helen was a nurse before she retired, she is an avid gardener. I had never heard of a butterfly vine, but Helen explained to me that, not only does the vine have beautiful yellow blossoms, but after the blossoms bloom, they take the shape of a butterfly. She showed me both the blooms and the butterflies. Amazing!

Later in the day Helen goes to her Painting class. She considers herself a beginner but showed me a lovely watercolor she is painting, resembling part of her son's woody area with a pond and waterfall. She is using a photograph of the area as her guide. A new challenge for Helen in her eighties.

In the afternoon Helen and Keith like to go to the community indoor pool where they exercise their legs and relax their bodies. But … the best part is yet to come. Around 4:30 p.m. Helen and Keith hold court on their patio with a "cocktail party" for their neighbors. This is a daily occurrence for close neighbors who look forward to it. It's a great time for snacks and drinks and just good conversation before dinnertime. After dinner, at approximately 9:00 p.m., it is time to retire. It's been a good busy day. Good night!

Next, we visit with Esther. Esther has just turned 91 but that hasn't slowed her down much. She moved to the retirement community with her husband three years ago. Sadly, he passed away last year. She gives us a peek at some of her days in a typical week. In her own words:

"Monday: My daughter, who lives in another city, spent Sunday night with me. We were up about 7:30 a.m., dressed, made the beds, had breakfast, and then went to the grocery store before she went home. I read the paper and gave it to my neighbors as they are not from the area and I like to share.

"After lunch I made sure all was picked up, then I worked at my desk for a while and checked my e-mail. I relaxed the remainder of the day as I was tired.

"Not an exciting day, but a satisfying day. Some work and some relaxing enjoyment.

"Tuesday: The early hours are about the same, except that I have an exercise class in the morning. After dinner there is an evening class to study 'Music through the ages.' We finished this series and now we will study 'Mythology.'

"Thursday: My other daughter and I met my son in the Galleria area to transact some business. We had coffee and visited a bit before going our separate ways. (Ed. Note: Esther still drives her car)

"My daughter and I stopped for a sandwich before coming back to the apartment where she helped me make a few changes ... before she went home. I relaxed the remainder of the day reading and knitting.

"Saturday: Up at the regular time, straightened the bedroom a bit, then to the kitchen for breakfast. I try to make Saturday special as it is a more relaxing day. So today it was a waffle, frozen of course, as I did not bring the big waffle iron when I moved here. Still it was good.

"Saturday is also the day I give my three flowering plants extra attention. One is an African Violet given to me by a friend when we moved here and it has nearly tripled in size during three years. Another is a Christmas Cactus which is a start from my grandmother's and is now nearly 60 years old in my care. It has been with me, living in Indiana, New Jersey, and Texas. I have not always had a good place for it, and it did not grow much for several years. I have a good window now, and it has really grown. I wish my grandmother could see it, but maybe she knows. The third plant is a Leather Plant, also known as Closet Plant, which three of my grandchildren gave me when my husband died last year. It gives me a good feeling as I take care of my plants. No, I do not talk to them, just give them TLC.

"Sunday: This Sunday I will have my usual morning schedule, except no time to read the paper, as the church bus picks me up, along with a couple of residents, to go to church. I return in time for Sunday Brunch, then read the paper, and possibly take a nap. Evenings vary, as one Sunday it is a DVD of a Broadway Hit, and another Sunday it is a DVD of an opera. This month it is *Madame Butterfly* by Puccini. Next Sunday we'll listen to a concert given by a young upcoming pianist.

"There is always an activity going on here and lots of people take part. I am one of them. Some are educational and some just fun, and a good way to get acquainted."

Age certainly has not slowed Esther down. Remember Betsy? She explained in an earlier chapter why she enjoys living in her chosen retirement community. Betsy just turned 75. Here she tells us what a day in her life looks like:

"I have made my life as easy and stress-free as possible since retiring from the workplace. A day in my life is pretty much whatever I want it to be.

"On Saturday mornings I bowl in our wii® bowling league (digital bowling on the internet), but, every other morning I get up whenever I wake up. I eat breakfast, then go into the 'Bistro' (a common area where residents gather for coffee and conversation – doughnuts on Fridays). I enjoy discussing the news of the day and learning true life stories and experiences of fellow residents.

"From there, I go to our in-house library to volunteer my services. I prepare new books for shelving. I am an avid reader, so it's nice to help in that way.

"Then it's lunchtime. I usually have lunch in my apartment. If shopping is not on my agenda, I spend most of the afternoons with a good book or catching up on chores; except on Sunday afternoons, when I play gin rummy with friends.

"Many evenings I have cocktails with friends in one apartment, or another, or in the lounge/bar area. Then it's a lovely gourmet dinner in our formal dining room. It's an early evening. I'm usually home by 7:30 or 8:00 p.m. Saturday night is the exception. I go out for live music and jive until midnight with a 'young' male fellow resident who loves to dance as much as I do. My life is good every day. I am a happy lady."

Thus far we have introduced you to a number of ladies, ages 75-91. Another resident is a very busy gentleman, John, a retired engineer. He explains that he is "mobility challenged" and uses a motorized wheel chair. His wife has been diagnosed with dementia and needs help. John refers to his condition but does not allow it to keep him from a full and exciting life. He is truly a super-senior. You will read more about his story in a later chapter, "Coping with Illness."

3

Relationships

From the day we are born we form relationships. A new baby looks to his mother for comfort. The toddler finds an adult or another toddler to be with. All of us find a "best friend" as we grow from kindergarten to elementary school, middle school, high school, and on to college. It's part of growing up! We form relationships, expand them, change them, but never do without them.

As we reach the seventies and above, our relationships seem to become even more important. No one wants to be alone. We find that some of the friends we have made in the past have gone their own way while others may have changed their interests. Hopefully, we have our families who want to nurture us and take care of us. We notice, however, with some surprise, that the relationship has changed. While we were in charge in our younger years, some of us may be expected to follow our children's desires, and often those desires don't match what we want for ourselves. We realize that this is the time when we have to make decisions. This is the time when living in a retirement community becomes a definite possibility. We need a place where we can be free and independent, and where we can look forward to the visits from our family and friends. These visits will be special treats for us and for them, but these visits will be on our terms. There will always be some who prefer to be dependent, but the majority of us will cherish this time in our lives and our new place in society, where we can make the choices for ourselves.

I have discussed this subject with a number of residents on our "campus." Many came here because they wanted to "downsize." They were tired of keeping house, worrying about all the details of home maintenance, fixing meals, tending a large garden, and general day-to-day care of the home.

Shirley explained her decision to move here. "This is the first time that I'm free enough to do many things I enjoy. When my husband passed away, I felt lonely. I missed having a partner. Here I have taken up line dancing and I love it." Not only has Shirley enjoyed the dancing, but she has also found a partner.

Sally and Harry have had an exciting life together for more than 60 years. After Harry retired at 59, and the children were in college, they gave up their home, and moved into a motor home as their permanent place of residence. They lived their dreams, as they traveled in the motor home all over the United States. When in the Western states, they took time out to go on cruises to Hawaii, and other far away places. When in the East, they visited Europe. "We got better airfares that way," they explained. Twenty-five years later, they donated the motor home to their favorite charity, and moved into our retirement community. They were ready to settle down. Sounds like the ideal solution, doesn't it? They have slowed down a bit, now that they have reached the eighties, but they are still independent, and doing what they want to do.

Catherine is 76. She is single, has never been married, and has always been independent. She dresses beautifully and makes friends easily. Within the community she has found a smaller circle of friends. I see them meeting before dinner, then going to dinner together, and perhaps spending the evening playing games, or just enjoying each other's companionship.

Evelyn has a son in Texas and a daughter in Minnesota. She lost her husband of more than 60 years, and still misses him. Realizing her plight, one of her neighbors gave her a kitten, now her constant companion. Her second delight is forming a good relationship with the staff member, who arranges trips for the residents.

Being new to Texas, Evelyn has learned more about the state than most Texans know. She participates in every excursion that is available. She also travels back and forth, to see her daughter and grandchildren in Minnesota. When she is gone, a neighbor takes care of the cat.

Relationships can be formed here in so many ways. In this community, the dining hours are arranged so that people are seated as they come in. They can come in with friends and sit together, or they can arrive singly or in doubles, and be seated with others. What a wonderful way to meet new residents! Dining time becomes social time.

The many activities that are available in most residential communities, lend themselves to forming new relationships. People who love to read, can join the book club. Exercise is a wonderful group activity. Bridge and other card games create good companions. I've mentioned line dancing before. There is something for everyone.

We have a Spanish class that is very popular. It's never too late to learn a new language. I am the Spanish teacher, a former high school teacher and administrator, and I volunteer my time for this purpose. It has given me a tremendous amount of joy, to work with a group of bright, intelligent people, who still love to learn. I don't have to urge them to do their homework. They do it before I ask. They also have fun doing it. When they first came to class, I gave each a Spanish name. For example, Patricia became "Pepita." She uses it every time I see her, in and out of class. One of my students has a parrot. She has informed me proudly that she has taught him to say "ola" in addition to his "hello." I love it, and they love it. It's a win-win for all of us.

I don't want to omit another important relationship that might develop between male and female residents in a retirement community. Many of us are here because we have lost a mate. Then some of us lose a mate, after we have made the move. After all, many of us have reached the ripe age of 80. Illness takes its toll also. Nevertheless, we live on, and our urges live on with us. I have seen many couples emerge in the four years I have lived here. Last year we had a wedding, and everyone was invited. The bride and groom had known each other many years ago, and met again when they, independently, moved to our "campus." Incidentally, each had a dog. Now the family has two dogs.

Ole moved here with his wife. They were devoted to each other. She had a car accident and unfortunately did not survive it. Ole was grief-stricken. For months we saw him moping around, pining after his lost love. After a year or so, he finally started coming alive again and joined several clubs. He has become quite popular among the ladies. Now he seems to be much happier living here. We welcome him back to life.

These are just a few of the many examples of relationships that evolve in a retirement community. Perhaps the same thing would happen if these individuals lived alone, or with their children, but chances are, the process would be much longer, and not as satisfying.

Finally, writing this book has created a new exciting relationship between the two of us, as co-authors. We only knew each other from a distance. A common interest motivated both of us to undertake this project. It is a welcome challenge.

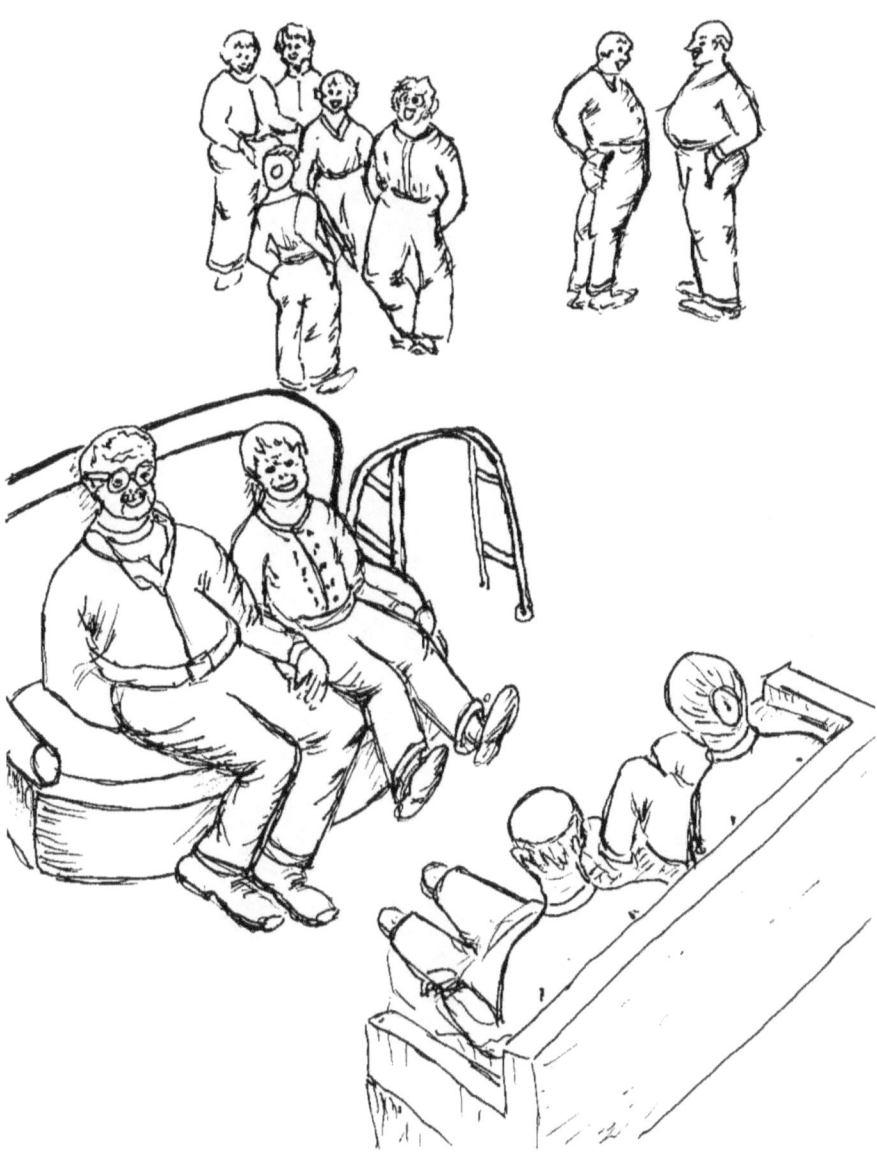

4

Changing the World One Favor at a Time

Catherine Ryan Hyde, author of the novel *Pay It Forward*, created a similarly named real life social movement, choosing this phrase as the movement's mantra. In Hyde's novel, a young boy is challenged by a teacher to design an activity that could change the world through direct action. In the boy's plan he inadvertently creates a charitable pyramid scheme. That is, when an individual responds to another person's desperate need for help of some sort, the recipient is told that nothing is expected in return except to find some way to help that person, passing on the unexpected good deed. The boy's first good deed indeed starts a stream of unexpected actions in Hyde's novel (and in the subsequent movie), initiating a growing real life movement of good deed doing known as "pay it forward."

How does that apply to our tales about members

of our "unique generation?" Although a penchant for charitable outreach activities undoubtedly characterizes the lives of many individuals throughout their lives, it often becomes more compelling and expansive at this time of life. It often expands quite naturally now, at a time when working for a living and immediate family responsibilities abate. This seems to have occurred especially prolifically among our super-senior population. Some doers may feel their contribution is merely civic duty, or just a sociable way of spending one's time. On the other hand, many look at these activities as a specific avenue in a higher scheme of life for giving back to the world around them for all the joys they've experienced in life. These "good deeds" that seem especially dedicated to paying it forward, we've found, range from low key, every day type of activities to some rather awesome projects.

An example of the former might be that of M.K., who in her late 80's has chosen to contribute to our recycling paper project by daily retrieval of the extensive trash mail that people immediately discard upon scanning their mail. On the one hand, this may seem little more than neatness to the nth degree because M.K. has become such a familiar sight among all of us as she faithfully and cheerfully carries out this activity. However, money retrieved from the recycling project in turn contributes to our student dining service workers' Scholarship Fund.

This activity seems to have given special purpose to M.K.'s life, even though she is involved in many of the community's other activities, and "hi, M.K." (yes, that's the name she goes by) is often heard in the hallways. On the other end of the continuum is a rather awesome project that seems to have taken on a life of its own. The core idea was initiated by Judy, whose professional occupation in the larger community had involved the sale of other's treasures, antiques and such. This project emerged as residents moved in with possessions, now often far beyond the capacity of their new apartments, who then willingly contributed the excess to a "good cause" rather than trying to sell or otherwise dispose of it. Judy took on the challenge of where in our new community we might store and display the now expendable items (an unused apartment), as well as generating a work force of fellow residents to serve as managers and sales people on a weekly basis.

Large and small possessions flowed in—from an antique piano to old jewelry, multiple furniture and art items, lamps and china collections. Soon other residents began to shop the treasures and found just the right piece for a blank space in their apartments; staff members, and even visitors to the community, also became intrigued buyers of unusual items of age and beauty. Income becomes part of a Benevolent Fund for residents who encounter financial setbacks, as well as adds significantly to the Student Scholarship fund---the pay it forward network powerfully in action! Judy's marketing skills have made this venture grow by leaps and bounds. It has become an especially successful avenue of pay it forward, not only for Judy, who by now wheels around the community in her Scooter, but also for the many other residents who now have become willing workers!

In a different vein of giving, Renate, who had been a lifelong, successful and innovative Spanish teacher to high school students, decided now to offer Spanish classes to fellow residents. While language learning is described in another chapter, Renate's venture fits well this theme of paying it forward since she has undertaken this task as a gift to those of us eager to learn Spanish. What an exciting time we have focusing on conversational Spanish, especially as it is set to music. (Her daughter had written and recorded special music to facilitate second language learning). Now many of us have begun to greet each other in the hallways, dining room, and everywhere—¡Hola! ¿Cómo estás? Muy bien, muchas gracias! We have become very vocal recipients of Renate's "giving back" spirit.

Then we have Keith, whose wife died about a year after they had moved into the community, who now brings so much pleasure to all of us by managing a delightful collection of music and other programs on our community's TV station. He has now become the videotaping specialist of events here in the community events to be played back for residents who hadn't been able to attend them. Even though many residents may be scarcely aware of his contribution, his quiet demeanor adds much to the concrete, real time pleasure of all!

Which brings us to yet another activity of paying it forward, this time to others in the community who for various reasons are in special need of comfort and social support at this time in their life. The Community of Hope was initiated by our Pastoral Ministry representative to become an instrument of special outreach to those fellow residents in need who haven't felt comfortable actively seeking help. Likely candidates to serve in this role of outreach are invited to first participate in about six sessions of guidance regarding effective ways to become caring listeners and responders while refraining from taking charge of the recipient's responses. Careful attention is paid to the private nature of all interactions. Their task is to be alert to notice residents who are experiencing these needs for caring interest, and to make themselves available through casual visits. They might find that the individual just needs one or two such visits to realize that someone cares about them, while some individuals need more sustained attention. Though a religiously diverse program, and proselytizing is definitely not a goal, a critical aspect underlying this particular program is to convey a generic god's love (as they, the givers, have already experienced it) through reaching out with caring, gentle attention to others.

Pay it forward activities in a community such as ours even continue their effect when some doers have completed their earthly journey. Elizabeth, one of our early residents had been a scientist at NASA in her professional life. I first knew her as she made her mark among us by being a very independent thinker and outspoken contributor to the discussions of our Bible Study group. But she really found her "pay it forward" life by taking on the role of mentor/teacher/friend to young boys in a nearby community facility for troubled boys. She went to the facility weekly to spend time with these troubled youth, encouraging other residents to join her. Since then others have become involved in mentoring youth in nearby schools, and other similar planned activities have become more frequent.

The activities described here are but a sample of what is happening in these special years of many of our super-seniors as they cheerfully pay it forward. While Warren Buffet and others are proclaiming intention to convert their surplus earnings to special charitable causes is a very visible and honorable "Pay it Forward" action, the quiet activities by our super-seniors, such as described here, are truly at the heart of superior deed doing PAYING IT FORWARD!

5

Extending One's Perspective

Ah Ha! Another fascinating evening begins for a group of super-seniors of the unique generation as they gather to ponder via television a selected short story, Broadway musical, historical fable, or a selection from some other genre. After watching a 30-minute DVD, delivered by a respected professor, they excitedly pounce on ideas and insights, even disagreements that have emerged, often challenging perceptions they have held since early college years and a lifetime of just living.

"Successful aging requires that people continue--- across their lifetime----to express a curiosity about their changing world, an ability to adapt to shifts in their developmental and physical capacities, and an eagerness to engage new perspectives, skills, and appetites." (*The Third Chapter. Passion, Risk, and Adventure in the 25 Years after 50 Sarah Lawrence Lightfoot, p.7*) But wait! We

are talking about a "unique generation," those years
AFTER 70!

The specific activity just described was initiated
when a curious Maisie brought forward an instructional
DVD she had unearthed that had caught her interest.
She persuaded energetic Donna to organize biweekly
meetings to investigate the heart and soul of famous,
short story literature. The group needed a recognition
tag. "Knowledge Seekers" was created by Jack, and
their search for new perspectives began. Enhanced bits
of wisdom generated from discussing musicals, with
insights about fables, following quickly. Others have
followed, including the study of mythology, and new
leaders have emerged.

But don't be misled, this is but one such search for
knowledge growth and new perspectives generated in
this residential retirement community of more than 500.
Other groups focused on Shakespeare, Great Decisions
political policy, opera past and current, and other topics
that will surely arrive soon or have already occurred
in a perhaps less obvious persona. As one participant
described the experience:

"What a fascinating literature-based topic to
ponder, as we do in our weekly Shakespeare group!
Each of us approaches with a different perspective for
understanding his poetic renditions of history of another
time than ours. And each of us with our own unique

penchant for the many flavors, nuances and possibilities that Shakespeare conveys in his wonderful tragedies and comedies, brings to our discussions unique insights and talents to enrich us individually as we travel through those seven ages Shakespeare describes.

One summarizes the facts and scenes with such succinctness and clarity that we gasp, "Oh, that's what Shakespeare's talking about". Another brings all the loose ends together into a neatly packaged grasp of the sense of a scene in the play. One explains the many language derivations that were so unique to middle century England and so important in Shakespeare's usage. One transforms our appreciation through emphasizing the beauty and grace in Shakespeare's poetic renditions, while still another attunes our ears to the auditory beauty of the spoken lines. Still another tries to draw the intricate connections between the multitude of characters. As we leave our brief evening with Shakespeare, we come away with exciting anticipation of our next session when we will again be enriched by the multitude of insights we've shared, and their applications to our own lives today. We are energized with the grateful realization that, "No, we have not yet come to Shakespeare's seventh age . . . mere oblivion". For we have been energetically enjoying our discussion of Shakespeare!

Speaking of the initiators of groups pursuing new

perspectives, it is interesting to note that Donna is highly involved in the informal government of the community, certain she never wants to leave this great setting, and so busily engaged that she leaves her dining companions with a wave, saying "Well, I'm off to an evening of poker." Maisie, who continues her pursuit of violin excellence with daily practice and Elderhostel attendance, initiated the Shakespeare play reading group, and still makes time to fashion an Admiral Nimitz memorial plaque on her husband's contributions during World War II. Jack and Jeanne enrich the company of all of us with their sense of humor and warm camaraderie, even as Jack retells a story from one of their sessions.

What does this have to do with each of us pursuing new perspectives? It portrays for these individuals and many others in this community a determination to engage in life, setting aside for the present their loss of life partners and their own various physical limitations in order to be relevant to the life after 70 generation and to the world. But most of all, their activities tend to be a vibrant example to that generation that follows—their offspring and their grandchildren.

6

Spirituality and Religion: Important Pursuits

"Spirituality is about the hunger in the human heart. It seeks...reason to exist that is beyond the biological or the institutional or even the traditional... Religion is about what we believe and why we believe it. It is about the tradition, the institution, the system." (*Called to Question: A Spiritual Memoir. Joan Chittister. Oxford: Sheed and Ward.2004*)

We are very fortunate that our beliefs are expected to be part of our individuality and a fundamental right. Religious diversity here is highly encouraged and developed in many formal and informal ways. This kind of environment has allowed many of us to continue, nay, to expand our conception of life, the world, and beyond, and our place in the universe; and, also, to enjoy the contributions we can continue to make in our unique time of life.

This approach underlines the fact that each of us is somewhere on a continuum from strict allegiance to a tradition and system of rules for guiding our lives (that is, *religion*), all the way to an individual and ever-expanding search for mystical dimensions of life which might differentially inform us on how we might shape our lives (that is, *spirituality.*) The activities to be described in this chapter provide opportunities, which individuals at any point on this continuum may choose to pursue. Only individuals can decide where they are on the continuum and how they will use the activities.

As an example: through a weekly prayer initiated early in our community's existence by one such resident, people of all belief systems have found special purpose and comfort. In fact, the initiator and a friend have come to be synonymous with comfort to all, even though participants with differing backgrounds who chose this activity have varied over the past five years. The group is expected to observe all the privacy rules of the community, plus it may not expose identities of prayer recipients without their specific permission. Extending from that beginning, a staff Pastoral Representative was appointed whose tasks included finding spaces and arranging times for other such groups to meet in this busy community. In fact, a Meditation Room has been set aside, available to individuals and groups who might want a quiet place to ponder spirituality alone or in a group.

This Pastoral Representative has facilitated an interdenominational Sunday service for those who choose to attend, or who are unable to travel to outside churches. They meet weekly, often with resident–invited local pastors as speakers. She has also arranged support for a Roman Catholic Mass to be celebrated monthly, and for weekly Shabbat services, along with a yearly Seder feast in one of our dining rooms.

Further activities have included arranging sets of classes to be taught via DVDs of the renowned Teaching Company® on the Buddhist, Christian, Judaic, and Muslim belief systems, and most recently on Hinduism. Occasionally, members of a particular faith group from the surrounding community have been invited to join in or lead a discussion. Thus, you can see that encouragement of diversity and possibilities for extension of the insight about our universe are definitely in evidence, with allowance for firm religious conviction, yet also for pursuit of spirituality.

Along these same lines of addressing both the religious and spirituality needs of our unique generation, a Jesus–centered Bible study group has been active since the beginning of this particular community. Its first leader very thoughtfully encouraged discussions about Biblical narrative, the differences between multiple versions, and the ways we might better understand how the ideas apply to us as individuals. When that leader left the community to serve particular family needs, a second leader, a church deacon, skillfully and creatively continued to guide our pursuit of Biblical knowledge. Again, we could each define where on the continuum from religious conviction to pursuit of spirituality best fit our individual need. Thus, our sessions abound with excited and sometimes passionate discussion!

Describing these various group activities, that especially promote or support the pursuit of spirituality and/or religion at this time in our unique generation years is not meant to suggest that a designated group is essential to the task. However, now that responsibilities for one's children or other family members have passed on to the next generation, we of the 70+ generation have become available for the *"passion, risk, and adventure"* touted by Lawrence–Lightfoot in her book, *"The Third Chapter."*

Though we may tamp down the passion, many of us "over 70s" enthusiastically accept risks and seek adventure as we resolutely pursue the mystical dimensions of life termed *"spirituality."* We may use diligent study, extensive reading, group discussions, relationships with other kindred souls, service activities, or even dinner table conversations. In any case, our lifetime of a rich variety of experiences leads us to believe that we now are enfolded in an ideally set stage for unraveling the mysteries of the universe!

7

Learning a Second Language

Research tells us that learning a second language is good for the brain. As we reach the age of the "unique generation," keeping our brain active becomes a major goal. Therefore, it is no wonder that foreign or second language instruction has become a popular activity in our retirement community. The old saying, "you can't teach an old dog new tricks" does not hold true for us. We are eager to go forth and learn more. We no longer need a special reason, although travel is still very popular with us and it doesn't hurt to be able to say "Buenos días," "Bon Jour," or "Guten Tag" when we reach our foreign destination. Learning a second language can really be fun. The trick is to find a teacher who considers it fun and a challenge. I like to think of myself as such a teacher. My trick is to teach language *with music.*

At our retirement community we have an active

group of super-seniors in their seventies and eighties who meet weekly to learn Spanish. We learn basic vocabulary with songs designed to teach the basics. Most of us like to sing but those who don't, chant. We listen to the songs and sing along. Again, research has found that music helps retain new knowledge, whether it's the old nursery rhymes we learned as youngsters, the commercial jingles we have heard and continue to hear on radio and television, or, in our case, the Spanish songs that teach useful vocabulary. I observe my students laughing, clapping their hands to the rhythm of the songs, and, above all, learning to communicate in the new language.

One of the most difficult things to teach is the vowel system in Spanish. Each vowel has one sound only, while in English there are a variety of ways to say *a* or *u* and others. In our class, we take the five vowels, *aeiou* and chant them to the rhythm of a conga line. We say – *a e i o u* – *hup* several times and we kick our legs when we come to *hup*. It's easier to remember that way. Those of us who are agile enough, can actually dance the conga line.

The students also take on Spanish names when they first join the class. That creates all kinds of merry laughter and stays with us. As I wander down the halls in our buildings, my students greet me with *"Hola, maestra, buenos días!"* while I answer *"¡Hola, Pepita!"* or

"¡Hola, Carlos"! Sometimes the students like to use their new Spanish names with everyone they meet. They've taken on a new personality.

When we become part of the "unique generation," many of us feel that we can lose some of our inhibitions and gain a sense of freedom that influences our actions. "Life should be fun, we have nothing to lose, no one to impress, we can be ourselves!" We are learning a new language because we enjoy it, not because we need it for a degree or for a job.

In our community a number of us have lived in foreign countries during our earlier years or were born there. That means that some of us are fluent in a second language. It's fascinating to learn about these residents and hear their many stories. Groups get together to practice their language to keep in practice. We have residents from South American countries, Europe and Asia. There is so much we can learn from each other. Now we have the time to do it. What a wonderful age the seventies and eighties can be!

8

Reading: Nurturing Mind, Soul and Body

"Reading is not simply an intellectual pursuit . . . it lights the hurricane lamp of self; that's why it survives." (*Quindlen, April 5, 2010, Newsweek.*) No matter what time of day at our community, one is likely to meet someone strolling down the hallway with one or more books in hand. No, this isn't a college setting—it's a lively senior living abode of individuals who had lived rich lives in various fields of endeavor. And these strollers may simply be on their way to his or her apartment to immerse self in a latest literary acquisition. Or, just as possibly they are on their way to one of the myriad of sources available for exchange and replenishment of their reading treasures. As Quindlen suggests, passionate readers feel strongly the need to keep their hurricane lamps well lit.

So where in this residential community are all

these sources for finding literary treasure? First of all, an incredible number of bookshelves have been tucked away in hallways across the entire residence area. On those shelves (volunteer-constructed by the woodworking super-seniors) are an impressive set of paperbacks contributed willy-nilly by residents wanting to clear their own bookshelves. One can imagine the diversity of content that multiple residents have downloaded to our community's shared collection—from romance novels, spy thrillers, and mysteries to westerns and travel narratives, as well as some traditional classics and even some spiritual guides as well! Residents can stop by when in need of a new piece and return their previously borrowed items. And Lois, besides being an available "pet-sitter and dog-walker" for many of her resident friends when they are away for a few days or are feeling under the weather, has become the official book shelf guardian. She is likely to be seen pushing a huge cart loaded with paperbacks to add new items or recirculate the books from one floor to another as people return their latest read.

Perhaps the central source of reading material for residents is an amazing 3000 or so volume library that emerged early in our history when this community's creators set the concept in motion. Accepted readily it became a reality due to the persistence and hard work of people such as Marilyn, Donna, and a whole slate of determined volunteers with multiple skills related to the needs of a library. After all, Marilyn's professional past included a special role as a university librarian who could effectively catalogue the myriads of selections from classics to encyclopedic volumes on topics from political leaders and movements, to art history, to famous philosophers, to current outstanding novelists. Donna, applying skills from her professional past recalls how much she liked doing all the things it took to assemble this library from scratch. Laughingly, she recalls how she was the only one who could lift the boxes of books! And then we have Nora, who specializes in covering some of the volumes with plastic to preserve them, and others who classify new selections, keep track of checkouts and returns, or plan cozy seating for those who just want to read the latest Wall Street Journal. The more than 3000 item collection and periodic new items provide a rich array of reading, and items are frequently on loan.

Knowledge about the various technologies to assist readers, who at this age are often experiencing visual difficulties, has supported access to large print scanners, as well as to a supply of large print check-out books. Even some audio-text and audio-tape items are available for borrowing. Some residents with further visual difficulties have also found a rich array of audio books that they can check out from a near-by library. A subscription to the daily Wall Street Journal and several weekly and monthly magazines, along with a cozy reading area promote highly agreeable daily library visits.

Recently, due to the large number of technical books contributed by incoming residents, four large boxes of serious textbooks, as well as literature items, were contributed to a local education program for parolees. The included items enriched the local program that could not afford them, though the program was initiated to help prepare these participants, who had abandoned schooling, for possible employment

However, the impetus for reading isn't limited to an impressive, entirely volunteer-activated library system. It is also an integral part of a book club initiated by Elizabeth who, along with 20 to 25 other residents, began a journey of book reviews shortly after this residential community had its beginning. One of the first books reviewed was *Reading Lolita in Teheran* by Azar Nariff. Patricia, who did the review, enhanced the session by serving Middle Eastern tea in traditional tea glasses she had brought back from her travels in Turkey. Elizabeth even wore a headscarf to demonstrate an item of clothing Middle Eastern women wear. Now this book and review notes occupy a time capsule that this community buried in the front lawn in memory of its first year of existence.

Five years later the book club is still going strong with reviews often enhanced by book-related items, such as a freshly baked potato peel pie brought by Marilyn to accompany her review of Shaffer and Barrows *The Guernsey Literary and Potato Peel Pie Society*. Or, circus music and peanuts to accompany Pat's review of *Water for Elephants*.

Of course, a number of residents continue to participate on a regular basis in the book clubs they belonged to before moving here. And we find ourselves often exchanging ideas about new books to review with daughters and friends from that earlier era. Which all goes to show the potency of Quinlen's "hurricane lamp of self."

9

Fabric, Artistry and Nimble Fingers

Within this amazing retirement community, a number of residents can be found who are nimble-fingered, gifted quilters. Some of them gather on Tuesday afternoons in the Creative Arts Studio to engage in this complex art in a social, relaxing atmosphere. Those who don't quilt do some other type of needlework, such as knitting or embroidery. This activity group, initiated by Cynthia early in our community's history in 2006, also takes special pleasure in the social aspect that has been associated with quilting from time immemorial.

As a unique example of this social aspect, this group became the avenue for myself (and others) to come to know the beautiful warmth of one early resident and to experience her deeply generous view of the world. Though I only had a couple of months of such sharing with her in our Tuesday sessions as she knit swaddling garments for lost newborns and quietly fought her own battle with cancer, I felt the breadth and depth of view she quietly exhibited as a special gift she gave to us all.

It becomes apparent that finished products become more than just works of personal satisfaction. They also become part of the outreach efforts undertaken by different groups who find ways to meet the needs of others in and beyond our community. Such outreach supports a Benevolent Fund for residents who have encountered financial woes, as well as a scholarship program for our student workers who contribute to the dining services. This group has also reached out to the Child Protective Services of this city and to other benevolent groups with their finished products. Some of the knitters in the group have also knit items for the hospital, and busily knit comfort and prayer shawls for residents in need.

A special example of an individual pursuing this kind of artistic endeavor is Betty. Her visual perspective, creative energy, and nimble fingers generate an endless array of wonderful products that are an inspiration for the rest of us. Betty has a particular gift for not only following complex pattern directions but also for improvising fabric gems at will. Seldom a week goes by that she doesn't have some newly finished product to share with the group. (We're not sure that her fingers ever sleep!) One such product, most memorable to me, was a Christmas quilt she made for our bazaar last year. My purchase of it not only added to the Scholarship Fund but also brought thorough delight to my young granddaughter, Caroline. She vividly showed that quilts are not just for bedcovers or wall hangings but also for comfort and joy.

One of Betty's most recent accomplishments was the restoration of a large, very old quilt patterned with delightful maids in sunbonnets, donated by another resident who was trying to organize her new apartment. Because of lengthy storage, the material had aged and become discolored in places. Through creative vision and clever practicality, Betty found ways to blank out discolored patches and obscure others with colorful embroidery and new edging. Thus emerged three beautiful smaller quilts just the right size for three children whom Child Protective Services will take under their wing, and whose faces will also reflect quiet joy.

This type of creative activity continues to drive Betty's pursuit of meaningful endeavors available to the unique generation. She was a fulltime homemaker in her previous life who did the obvious sewing many do for their families. After her children were grown, her daughter persuaded her to accompany her at a quilt-making workshop. Betty has been "hooked" ever since, filling her hours with such needlework when she and her hubby aren't off traveling somewhere. Through her creativity she keeps experimenting with all sorts of new ideas. She is so committed that she produces new pieces at breakneck speed almost weekly, if not daily (yet she doesn't convey franticness, rather an excited joy). She adds a zest to experimenting with new approaches and new tools, even purchasing a new kind of sewing machine with which she can create designs and accomplish new approaches to quilting. This is just one of the particular examples of activities that can come to characterize the life pattern of some of the super-seniors whom we have been trying to portray.

The works of other dedicated participants in this specific Quilting and Needlework group are too numerous to describe here. However, as an example of the further creativity in this arena of artistic pursuit, photos are included in a delightful scrapbook assembled by yet another member of the group.

As you can see, "nimble fingers" and spirited conversations enrich the days and needlework afternoons of many of the super-seniors at this residential community.

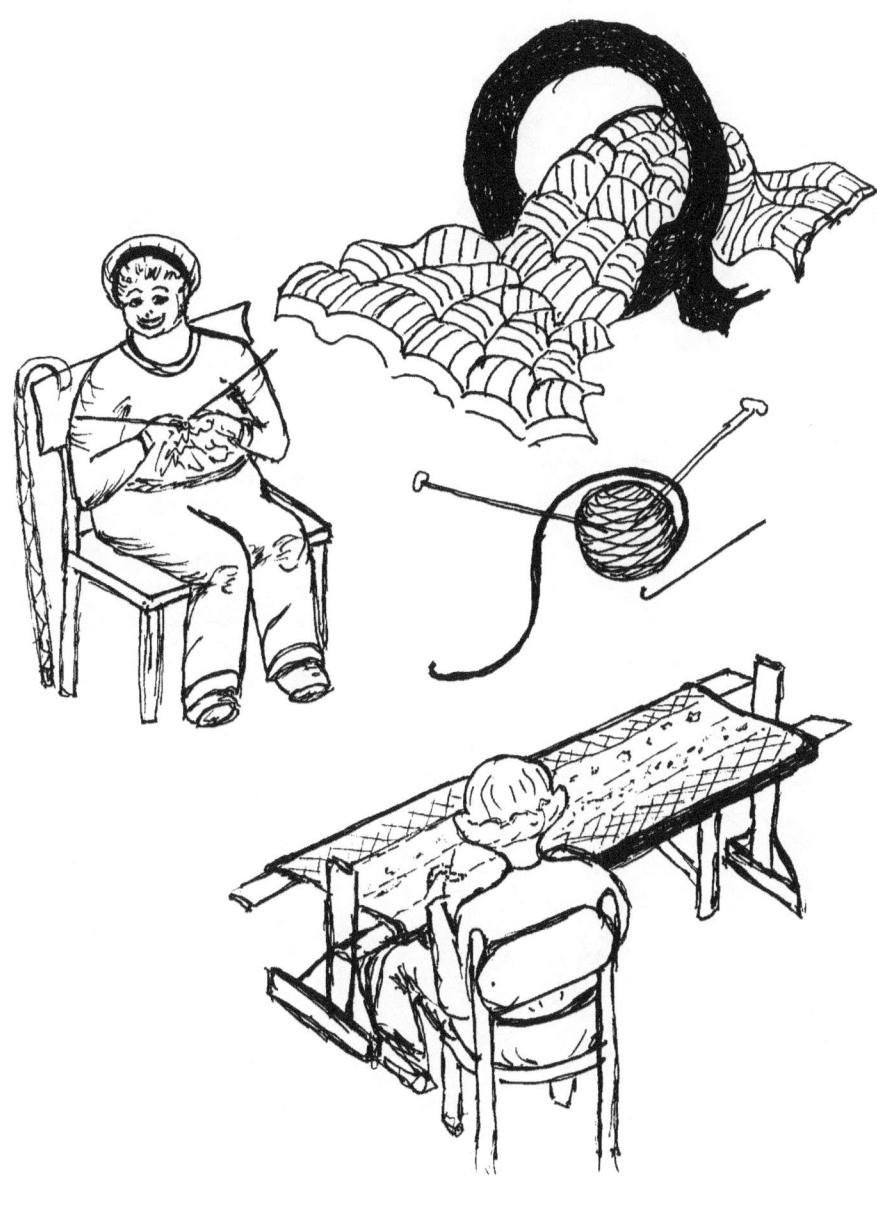

10

Painters, Poets, and Other Creators

Posted on a wall in the Creative Arts Room of this particular community-residents building are some of the recent works that the painting group members have been creating. They are beautiful, varied in style and content, and the work of both novice and more advanced artists. The artists, including Shirley, our illustrator, are super-seniors who have been making the most of this new time for self-expression. In this setting they are especially free to enjoy the encouragement of kindred souls, as well as the help and direction of available mentors. It is quite likely that each of these are seniors who are now initiating, or are recouping, a desire to create beauty with this medium, now that their responsibilities for professional work and family maintenance have been fulfilled. It is obvious from their demeanor that this is a special time for their special pleasure!

Among the population at this community, however, there are also individuals whose life work and life's pleasures included creating beauty through the medium of painting. Some of these artists continue to produce works for sale, for display among other artists' work, or just for the pleasure of continuing to be involved with their special talent. Beyond their own pleasure is often that of neighbors; for example, Geraldine almost always displays one of her works, as well as a number of different humorous displays, on the shelf outside her door. Thus, we all enjoy her artwork each day as we pass that door. Though of course I resist the urge, I have often been sorely tempted to snatch one of her beautiful horse paintings to give to my granddaughter!

Poetry may have once been considered the prerogative of a few people with unusual talent for assembling words and phrases in a musical or harmonious form that simply floats on the air. However, the writers and speakers of today's world are tending to express their ideas more often in poetic form, resisting the traditional grammatical and classical form. In this community of seniors, we seem to have a number of individuals who are drawn to poetry. Joy and Grant started and have continued to attract a small group of dedicated poets. Grant, himself, is about to publish yet another collection of his poems. This group meets once a week to read poetry and talk about its meaning and forms. Sometimes members read some of their own new poetry. There are, undoubtedly, many more individuals who choose to express themselves creatively through poetry––writing it, or reading it—even when they don't belong to a group.

There is much room in the lives of our super-seniors for expressing their creativity in many different ways. This is an ideal time to enjoy creative endeavors without the concern for monetary recompense. It is important, therefore, to encourage these creative abilities in ourselves and in those with whom we are spending our lives "reaching toward the heavens and for the stars!" Creativity of thinking and doing takes us beyond the hard work and serious considerations that usually governed our earlier life. Painting, poetry, and artistry of all forms, add music to our life's serious accomplishments!

11

Music Makes the World Go Round

"Come on and hear…come on and hear…Alexander's Ragtime Band…" It's Sunday evening and about 200 of our community of super-seniors have gathered in the living room to mutually enjoy, as is often the case, different programs of music, film, and the like. Jesse, a talented musician, grandson of one of the residents, just back from a year of study at Interlochen Music Camp in Michigan, is here to bring us "A Concert of Modern Ragtime," including a couple of his own compositions. We're even invited to "sing along" on one or two of the numbers! The hour is a special treat as we reminisce and rejuvenate to the sound of music with a rhythm from our past, and an overlay of the new and present from this musician of the future.

Music is an important part of the life of many of these super-seniors! Once a month on a Sunday evening, in fact, a group has sprung up who arrive at the living room to focus on a video presentation of a specific opera, from *Madame Butterfly* to Wagner's *Tristan and Isolde* or Mozart's *Don Giovanni* or others. Background information is first presented by a Teaching Company set of DVD's to help us better understand the particular production. On alternate Sunday evenings, Bill, the ambitious organizer of the opera sessions, has also been bringing famous Broadway musicals for our pleasure under the same Teaching Company® format. Some of those musicals we especially enjoyed in our past are *South Pacific, Sound of Music,* and others which have again burst forth to set our toes tapping and our voices wanting to join in with the music.

In a different vein of participation, a group of want-to-be singers, under the baton of Jim, a young-at-heart leader, join together every Friday morning to sing favored vocal selections and learn new ones, but also to rehearse selections for community events. Their presence has come to be sought after for these events of remembrance, of celebration, and other special occasions. Participation in this activity becomes cherished, even by those whose voices may be strong while their bodies have begun to require them to be the sitting members of the chorus. The sound produced is not diminished nor distorted by such physical adaptations, but, in fact, transmits joyous courage to the community of listeners.

Obviously, an accompanist is often needed for choral events. Some residents, such as Mary, have retained such skills learned earlier in life. They appear to relish their role accompanying vocal efforts at their local churches, as well as here in our residential community. David, whose professional engineering career had been supplemented with active piano performances in night-event groups since age seventeen, now often plays for all of us at special events. He continues to bring musical pleasure to this, his adopted community, with his piano talent and skills. Although less visible, it is said that there are a few "closet" horn players among us who occasionally allow those instruments to again have voice.

Our collection of super-seniors includes some who continue their previous life accomplishments in the field of music by enlivening their current apartments and, inadvertently, our entire community. Friends are occasionally allowed to be auditory recipients of these beautiful sounds. One such dedicated senior, Maisie, who had been a concert violinist with the New York Philharmonic in her earlier life, practices almost daily in her apartment overlooking the beautiful scenery of the setting sun and the lovely landscape outside.

Maisie has, as well, been part of a temporary volunteer program to assist adults who had not had the opportunity earlier in life to indulge in playing a musical instrument, at least not in a serious orchestral group. The current project was designed to teach adults who want to take up this activity now in their super-senior years just for the joy of experiencing music and expanding their life by growing a new skill! Our violinist also takes much pleasure in encouraging and mentoring an interested granddaughter who has even been exploring some modern jaunts into the world of music by summer performances at county festivals. So, we see our super-seniors bridging gaps between the generations even while their hearts and minds are forging forward.

Yet another form of music-oriented activity, one mentioned in the exercise chapter, is line dancing. As one individual who loves dancing mentioned, now that her marriage partner is no longer available, line dancing gives her an outlet for engaging in this thrill of physical expression of music. It's an avenue for growth in this setting with other life-oriented seniors.

Musical expression seems to bring out the divine in our bodies and souls and minds in many different ways. Music does indeed make the world go round!

12

Woodworking Beauty and Imagination

As he walked down the hall, carefully swinging a just completed small, bright yellow airplane, this tall gentleman morphed into a young lad (in my mind, just as in today's television magic epics), about to see if he might fly his plane to the moon. "After all, space travel might be in my future," the little boy in him might have been delightedly musing. But no, this was one of our unique generation's representatives in this retirement community who have taken to expressing their newly resurrected creativity through woodworking and related projects. This particular yellow airplane was one of nine he had constructed to delight the playtime of children in the city's Child Protective Services, along with that of one or two grandchildren.

Dan is part of a group who recouped a space to be dedicated for woodworking or other such projects by men (and some women) who had been too busy in their working chapter of life to bring their creative handwork into focus. Although this is a rather loosely organized group, Ray is instrumental in making sure that they have all of the possible space that community executives can reserve for this group. Members have keys to their gathering space, which allows them to come at any time that they wish to work on a project stored there. For example, Jim reports that the mood to construct sometimes comes at odd times, even when he wakes up at 4:30 in the morning. Ray can often be seen carrying one of his partially constructed projects under his arms as he walks the hallways to the shop or back to his apartment.

In the shop, members of the group can store both the tools that they work with, as well as their unfinished projects. The projects have been varied, ranging from a polished stand for supporting quilts in the making, (that is now in the needle worker's special domain) to doll beds and furniture, again for Child Protective Services (with needle workers in partnership crafting the stuffed dolls and bedding).

A few such projects appear to cross the line from toy to cherishable replica for the future of 21st century construction and transportation equipment. These include Jim's grand miniature backhoe, and even some wooden trains, carefully crafted and lovingly painted.

We envision that, in the future, they will be looked on with the same wonder that we apply to antiques we seek to collect today. We will say, "do you remember when trains like this rumbled across our country?" I could have stood and looked for hours at that marvelous backhoe displayed in the craft window! Its creator, Jim, musing about why and how this activity had become such a passion for him in his fourth chapter of life, recounted how he had started to do such woodworking in his early boyhood, encouraged and appreciated by teachers and family. This became a hobby that continued throughout his adult life as a professional engineer and father of a family. Now, at age 87, his enthusiasm for this hobby is very contagious!

Jim also talked about another product of his hobby, that of re-finishing furniture, his own as well as that of an occasional neighbor who doesn't want to lose a favorite table or cupboard. As a matter of fact, Keith (who also is our communications expert providing an array of music for our TV station) is also fond of furniture rehabilitation, and often does such projects for others who don't want to discard a piece they treasure.

While we speak in such esoteric terms about these woodworking projects, the projects more often become a special treat to some child who, in turn, can play and dream simultaneously about being such an engineer of the next generation! Thus, recently, a collection of fifty or so such toys was sent off to Child Protective Services to be distributed to children in need of such special dreams! Jerry, another member of the group, has been a special advocate for these children.

Not all of the crafted works are purely wood constructions. Patrick seems to find joy in glasswork and has found pleasure in helping others acquire the art of doing this kind of activity. His beautiful glasswork plaques often grace the entrance to their apartment, usually reflecting the theme of the month, such as a pumpkin or goblin at Halloween time. These plaques have also been displayed in one of the common hallways for all to see and enjoy.

You can see that extension of our creative capabilities to new genre and new venues can provide exciting opportunities for meaningful work, growth, and gift-giving at this time of our lives. After all, these are the super-seniors of the unique generation!

13

Exercise for Physical and Mental Health

"When you don't use it, you lose it!" Haven't we heard this said all of our lives? Well, it's truer than ever when you reach our age, the seventies and beyond. People, both men and women, have a tendency to become couch potatoes after they retire. However, it is different when you move into a retirement community. The opportunity to exercise is there. All you need to do is take advantage of it. And it can be fun too.

At our community, there is an exercise room with stationary bikes, treadmills for walking and machines for stretching. Television sets are mounted above the treadmills so that you can keep up with the world while you are walking at a speed that's right for you. Trained personnel can provide us with a personal exercise program, designed for each individual. They also supervise individual exercises to give us a goal to reach or to help us get well when we break down from time to time. As I walk by and pass the exercise room, I see some interesting things. One resident is reading a book while his legs are pedaling. Another is walking as fast as he can as he watches the news of the day above him. Two ladies are carrying on a swift conversation as they play with a huge ball to exercise their arms.

Water exercise is very popular and encouraged for all participants. In our community there are scheduled exercise classes as well as informal individual water activities. Not only is swimming and moving your limbs good for the body but it also becomes an excellent vehicle for forming friendships.

I believe my favorite exercise is tai chi. Before moving here, I had heard of tai chi but never considered taking part in it. It's an ancient art with flowing movement to reduce strees and improve health. It is sometimes described as "meditation in motion" because it promotes serenity, connecting the mind and body. Originally developed in ancient China for self-defense, tai chi evolved into a graceful form of exercise that's helpful in a variety of health conditions. We do a number of movements, each with a label or purpose, such as good for arthritis, good for the heart, good for your back, etc. In my case, I have a little bit of all of these symptoms. For some reason, as I practice tai chi, I feel better. I guess the Chinese know something we don't.

Not only is tai chi good for you, it is also a lot of fun. I'll admit, we are not at an age where we look particularly graceful as we are doing our swaying and turning, but we do it together and there is some visible symmetry.

As I've stated before, tai chi is good for the body. It's great for the mind too. We do what's called "forms." Each form has a number. Form #1 consists of a number of movements. The movements for #2, #3, #4 and #5 resemble each other, but vary in complexity. As we do the movements and listen to the instructions of our teacher, we learn the names of these movements. There is supposed to be some similarity between the name and the movement, but for some of them you really need to use your imagination as well as your analytical mind. For example, we learned to "carry the ball." That's all well and good, but there is no ball. We shape our hands around an imaginary ball and walk with it. I love "carry the platter," a movement where we raise our hands together with the palm of one on top of the other. "Horse's mane" simulates stroking a horse's mane as we walk forward. I hope you get the picture. Another one that really tries my imagination is "squeeze the cheeks." This consists of pressing your "derrière" (butt, if you don't know your French) together to walk straight and erect. It's wonderful for a droopy back. Our instructor confided in us that this is the position required for

Brazilian models when they walk across the aisle. Try it! I could go on and on about tai chi, but I believe you get the idea.

Incidentally, tai chi is popular with both men and women. In addition to the standing tai chi, there is the sitting version, popular with those of us who don't stand very well. Many of us need help with balance, and there is no better way to get it!

Along with the active exercises, many of us enjoy the more sedate versions. One that's making a big hit at our retirement community is wii® bowling. We have six teams now who compete and take pride in their scores. A great way to exercise your arms and legs relaxing between taking turns.

Of course there is the availability for the best exercise of all – walking. There are private, well-kept grounds at many retirement communities. To keep active, we find time to walk alone, with our new-found friends, or with our dogs. We walk outside when the weather is good, or inside when it's cold or rainy.

One valuable thing we have learned as we have become part of the unique generation – it's important to exercise daily in order to remain healthy.

14

Let's Play a Game ...

Do you like playing games? Do you like the company of others who enjoy the same fun activities? Move to a retirement community. Here you will make friends quickly who love to gather either during the day or evening and will be quick to invite you to participate in a variety of games.

On a typical evening, after dinner, you will find a number of tables of different sizes, each with a group of residents busy at their game, either quiet in concentration or laughing out loud. Not being familiar with a number of these games, I visited some of the tables. The first one consisted of two women, deep in concentration, playing Rummikub®. Rosa and Bessie explained to me that this board and tile game takes a lot of thought and is really good for the brain.

The next table held six people, both men and

women, all laughing and talking while they played. "What game is this?" I asked. "Mexican Train" said Betty-Lou, one of the enthusiastic players. "We love it," she said, "because we have fun, but at the same time we can socialize!" Obviously this board game did not need a lot of concentration.

Another large table, with eight people, was engaged in a board game with holes in the board. Marty explained to me that it was named "Jokers Wild" and affectionately called "Social Security."

Of course there are numerous card games, such as gin-rummy and bridge, for those who want to concentrate completely. Bridge lovers will find tables for beginners (and sometimes lessons) and there is duplicate bridge for the aficionados.

In one corner of the large living room where these games are held, there is a large puzzle available for anyone who wants to spend a few quiet minutes or longer, adding a few pieces at a time.

A night of Bingo is available for those who like to play this popular game of chance. The proceeds go to a worthy cause.

One of the most popular activities in our retirement community is wii® bowling on the television screen. This game started maybe a year ago and now has 6 teams and allows bowlers to participate in contests. For those of us who can do limited exercises, this game is a godsend. It allows you to stretch your muscles, concentrate on the bowling pins set before you, and hope for a "strike." If you have ever bowled in a regular bowling alley, you know the exhilarated feeling you get when you hit those bowling pins. Here you get the feeling without the pain.

If you are interested in something more vigorous, ping-pong is available. Just find a partner and go for it.

Why should you include game availability in your choice of retirement community? Of course they provide entertainment and a chance to mingle with others. They are a means for meeting new people and making friends. Most important though, they provide fodder for the brain, and all of us, super-seniors, cannot get enough of that.

15

Coping with Illness

Illness is bound to catch up with us – sooner or later. We, the super-seniors, 70 or older, are certainly more susceptible than our children and grandchildren. We don't have a choice in the matter. However, we do have a choice in how we cope with it when it strikes. No matter what happens to us, we can remain cheerful or fall apart. It is so much easier for us to be cheerful when we live in a retirement community. It is surprising to find fellow residents who have suffered as you have, who are survivors, and who are there to tell you: "Cheer up, you'll get over it, it's a piece of cake!"

Recently I was diagnosed with a malignant cancer on my cheek and had to undergo radiation treatments. This included marking my face with a thick crayon in various colors to give a road map to the radiology technicians to treat the appropriate sections of my cheek. Most people can hide the marks on their bodies with clothing but not I – I was marked like Zorro, for all to see. Pretty depressing, from my point of view. But, lo and behold, as a marked woman I stood out in the crowd. I discovered that almost half of the residents of this retirement community were survivors. I heard innumerable stories about the treatment, what it would entail, how I would feel, how long I'd be a marked woman and so on. I felt important and well loved by so many. What a feeling of relief. All were with me to cheer me on. I had a hilarious experience outside of my community. I visited the neighborhood grocery market. As I returned to my car to load the groceries, a young clerk stopped and looked at me with a big grin on his face. "I love what you did to your face!" he exclaimed. "Did you do this for the Superbowl?" How could I feel sorry for myself after that? Naturally I shared it with all my friends and all of us had a good laugh.

Let's get serious again. Illness comes to all of us at some time or other. One of the reasons we are here is that *we* want to feel secure, and that *our families* want us to be well taken care of and secure. A well-chosen retirement community can give us this feeling of security and can provide for us when the need arises. We have special staff members who have been trained to be first-providers. They come to your apartment the minute they are called. Our health statistics have been previously filed and can be forwarded to a hospital when necessary. There is a medical staff available to us at all times. I know of several cases where a life has been saved through the quick action of one of those staff members. Our families can rest with ease.

Let me introduce you to Evelyn. She has had a bad back as long as I have known her (approximately four years), but a few months ago she fell and broke her hip. After her return from rehabilitation, she needed an aide as well as a wheelchair. She has had some interesting aides. Since I live in the same building, I have had a chance to observe first hand the aides, as well as their effect on Evelyn. She has no family and has never been married. The aides, who have been approved by the management of the retirement community, have been both male and female. She seems to form a friendship with each one and her disposition has changed from a sad face, when she returned, to a happy and even radiant face. Her last aide was a handsome young man from Viet Nam and we could see that he was one of her favorites. She has enjoyed his solicitude and relished the companionship he gave her.

Margie has a short memory. So do many of us. In her case, it is important that she take her medicine to help her with every-day-living. Her family decided to contact the pharmacist at our facility, to make sure Margie gets her medicine. Every morning she visits the pharmacy, gets her pills, then sits down with a small group to have her coffee and of course the pills. She feels at ease, and so does her family.

Some of our residents are "mobility-impaired," the new expression for not being able to walk. Our hallways are wide enough so that individuals can comfortably zoom along to get where they are going. Of course that's the other advantage of living here. Many super-seniors have given up their cars. Here everything is under a roof. Although there are several buildings, they are all connected and accessible.

We consider ourselves fortunate. We never need to suffer alone. There is always someone with whom we can share, if we wish. At our age, we should accept help when it is offered. We deserve it.

I had a hard time at first, asking for and accepting help. Now I do both. Why did I change? Blame Kathryn; she was my aunt. Sadly, she passed away last year at the age of 94. When she turned 85, she came to visit me. Her home was in Utah. I live in Houston. Back in those days, we were still allowed to wait for passengers at the airport terminal where they exited from their plane. I had arrived about 15 minutes before the flight came in and waited patiently. When the gates opened, I watched for Kathryn. All the passengers passed me and no Kathryn. I started worrying and wondering what had happened to her. Finally the pilots exited the plane. I asked one of the flight attendants if there was anyone left on the plane. She thought for a minute and then she said that there was a "little old lady" waiting for a wheelchair. I was aghast. Kathryn had not told me she needed a wheelchair. Finally, she alighted in the wheelchair, an attendant guiding her gently into the waiting area. I ran over to her, gave her a light kiss on the cheek, and asked her what had happened. She ignored me and asked the attendant if he was sure he had all her bags. Then the three of us proceeded to the baggage room, with the young man and my aunt in the lead, waving aside any persons who dared get in their way. I became more and more worried.

When we reached the baggage room, the attendant retrieved Kathryn's suitcase, and whisked her out into the street. I was following behind as fast as I could. He finally stopped and asked me to move my car to a no-parking zone where Kathryn could be seated comfortably and without hassle. I did as I was asked. Kathryn thanked him politely and off he went. I entered the car and started the engine. We made a fast exit and soon were on our way home. I couldn't hold myself any longer. "Kathryn, tell me now what's wrong with you. Why are you in a wheelchair?" She looked at me sweetly and said: "Nothing is wrong with me. At my age, I deserve to have people take care of me."

To make this story short, Kathryn stepped out of the

car by herself, walked up the stairs and, throughout her visit, proved to be an excellent walker and companion. When she completed her visit, I took her to the airport and she immediately reverted to her position as an invalid. A smart lady!

Coping with a partner's illness is another type of challenge. It has become a specialty for John. Here is his story, in his own words:

John's day: "It's 7:45 in the morning and ringing of the telephone has wakened me from a very comfortable sleep. It is Allison, the lady from Hospice, calling to let me know that she will soon be here to give my wife, Martha, a bed bath. Allison does this twice a week. She calls about fifteen minutes before she will arrive at our apartment so that I will be ready when she does get her. (I would really enjoy another hour of sleep! But such is life, and I am glad to have Allison's services.) I have just enough time to arise and get dressed before she will be here.

"Years ago, before I retired, it was normal for me to arise at five in the morning on every work day. I arose, dressed, shaved, made and ate breakfast for myself, and was on the way to the nearby bus stop by six. I have certainly enjoyed a break from that routine—I really enjoy "sleeping in" every day; and on the days when Allison does not come, I will often sleep until nine o'clock or later!

"Now that I am up, I may be able to help Allison by getting Martha's daytime clothes ready to wear. And maybe I can help to move Martha in bed so that it will be easier for Allison to do her job. But, more importantly, I had better go to the kitchen to prepare breakfast.

"I have made breakfast in our home almost every day, especially on weekends, for most of the time we have been married—now over sixty years. But it's now a part of my daily activities because Martha has become less able to do many of the things which were once part of her normal routine. This decline in Martha's activities is part of her developing dementia. Fortunately, I am still able to do my bit. Our morning routine is really just that: a routine. We have cold cereal on Monday mornings, hot cereal on Wednesdays, cold cereal again on Fridays, eggs on Tuesdays and Thursdays, waffles on Saturdays, and often scrambled eggs, sausage, and a sweet roll or blueberry muffin on Sundays. Breakfast is ready by the time Martha is bathed and dressed.

"While on the subject of food, I might note that I also make our lunches. Some days, it will be soup and crackers; some days, I will fix BLT (bacon, lettuce, tomato) sandwiches or grilled cheese; some days, I will fix a tomato for each of us, stuffed with tuna salad; once in a while, I will buy an artichoke at the market, which we enjoy eating with mayonnaise after I have cooked it; I also enjoy fixing other sandwiches, such as ham and Swiss cheese on rye bread, egg salad, grilled peanut butter, or, one of my "specialties," an open-faced sandwich made by toasting a piece of bread, then grilling some cheddar cheese on the toast, then covering with sliced ham (followed by grilling), and finally topping with (and then grilling) a slice of tomato.

"I am somewhat hampered by being "mobility challenged." My legs have become weaker in the past few years and I now use a "power chair" to move around, particularly if I want to travel more than about ten or twenty feet. I do use a walker around the apartment, but if going to dinner in the main dining room or to any other part of our retirement complex, I use the power chair. In a way, I have become quite spoiled—it is really fun the "zoom" along in my chair at speeds greater than one can walk.

"Owing to Martha's condition, we are fortunate to have around-the-clock assistance, including during the middle of the night. Any time I need help, all I need to do is call, and the on-duty aide will come. These aides help Martha to get out of bed and into her wheel chair, to transfer from wheel chair to toilet and back, etc. Their help is much appreciated.

"Because we have such good help for my wife, I am able to indulge in the many activities of our retirement home—and there are many, indeed. There are opportunities to make new friends, to indulge in a variety of games (from bridge to Rummikub® to pinochle to dominos), we have two pool tables available, there is a well-equipped wellness center which has a host of exercise machines (and several wellness specialists and physical fitness trainers to help us in use of these machines) as well as a good-sized swimming pool.

"In addition to these activities for enjoyment, there are a variety of more intellectual activities available. This morning, I am going to attend a study group which is learning about some of the world's great religions. At this time, we are learning about Hinduism. I must confess that I had known little about Hinduism before now. I knew that it was widely practiced in India, but little else. Pastoral Ministries here at our retirement community had obtained a DVD on which were a dozen lectures on this religion by a college professor. Quite interesting!

"In addition to studies on the world's great religions, I am involved in several other rather intellectual activities. On Monday afternoons, I am part of a class of residents of our community who are trying to learn Spanish. This has been and continues to be a lot of fun. One of our residents was actively involved in the teaching of foreign languages in the local high schools, and she and her daughter have developed a delightful way to teach Spanish, making use of music (singing) to help in learning how to pronounce the language properly.

"On Tuesday evenings (three of the four Tuesdays of each month) I am involved in some other intellectual activities. On the second and fourth Tuesdays, we call ourselves Knowledge Seekers. At first, we read and heard lectures (via DVD) on a variety of short stories, starting with one by Edgar Allen Poe and continuing with stories written by other American authors, some Russian authors, etc. Just recently, we heard lectures (on DVD) on Great American Music: Broadway Musical, and we are shortly to embark on a series of lectures on Classical Mythology.

"On the third Tuesday evening of each month, I am involved in the Great Decisions program developed by the Foreign Policy Association. This is a program to learn about and discuss foreign policy problems which the U.S. faces in the world, problems ranging from our relations with Russia, to the current and recently past Global Financial Crisis, to questions about what has happened to the resolutions (the Millenium Resolutions) which were passed in about the year 2000 as the international community grappled with problems faced by poor but developing countries which need major economic assistance.

"I also attend monthly meetings of the Computer Group. We learn things at each meeting about how our computers work, how to solve operating problems we have encountered, etc.

"Finally, although I have not been very active, I am a member of the Woodworking Group. We have a large and very well equipped shop, with a wide variety of power and hand tools. One of the major activities of the group is making toys to donate each year to Children's Protective Services for distribution to needy children. The toys which are made include trucks, trains, and boats for boys as well as doll beds for little girls. I really need to get more involved with this group—to do my part!

"In view of the many activities here in our retirement community, I have little opportunity to get bored! And I haven't even mentioned activities in which I am involved such as the Dining Services Committee, which meets twice each month to make suggestions to those in charge of the kitchen which might help to improve our food service.

"At times, I think back to the period when Martha and I were thinking about possibly moving to a retirement community. We had been quite comfortable and happy for many years in our own home, in a delightful and pleasant subdivision. We lived there for forty-three years and we had made changes throughout the house so it was quite convenient, comfortable, and thoroughly fitted our style of living. And we had revised the landscaping, renovated the swimming pool, and done a wide variety of other things around the property.

"In addition to our city house, for thirty years, we

had owned a small (61-acre) farm, about two hours' drive west. We had spent most week-ends in those thirty-three years at the farm, restoring an old farm house (built over 100 years before we bought the farm), building and mending fences, fishing in our two ponds, entertaining guests, and generally enjoying a relaxing life. We had finally realized that we were no longer able to take care of the farm, and we had sold it about a year before we finally made the decision to move to a retirement community.

"When it came to selecting a retirement community, we had a variety of nearby places from which to choose, as well as places which might have been closer to either one of our two daughters (both of whom lived quite far away). Our final choice of this community involved several components:

"We knew several of those who already lived there (this was true of other nearby retirement communities, however).

"We liked the life style: the community was large enough so that it could support a wide variety of activities, some of which I have described above, and the living conditions appeared relaxed but well maintained. The life style did not appear to be too formal; for example, we appreciate being able dress informally.

"There became available an apartment which suited our wishes in terms of number of bedrooms, facilities available in the apartment (we have a large utility room in addition to the living room, kitchen, eating areas, etc.). The staff of the community all appeared friendly and outgoing.

"Our impressions of the food and eating facilities which are available were favorable. For example, there are two different eating areas, one an informal café and also a more formal dining room.

"The grounds were reasonably spacious; one does not feel crowded by the neighbors. The grounds are well maintained and tastefully landscaped—pleasant to see.

"Having decided to move here, and looking back… I think we made a good choice. We have certainly been comfortable and well supported. And the other residents have proved to be delightful as well as wonderfully varied."

16

Gardening and the Landscape:
Linking Earth and Beauty

Are you one of those special people who love nature and are passionate about gardening? Are you living in a home surrounded by greenery and beautiful flowers that you have planted? Do you wake up every morning just waiting to go outside to see what's new in your garden? Do you have a small plot where you grow vegetables and herbs and take pride in offering them to your family or friends during meal times or beyond?

There are many of us who fit into this category. We don't want to leave our homes because we'll miss this communion with nature. Well, it doesn't have to be this way if you choose your retirement community carefully. Many of us live on the first floor and have a small patio in front or behind our door. Around the patio there is an area with bushes and room to grow flowers. Even if we don't live on the first floor, our community management has designated a small plot of land exclusively for the use of residents to plant whatever they wish. Each resident who is interested in gardening chooses a plot of land. It's exciting for us gardeners to visit this plot and admire flowers, vegetables, vines and fruit, growing together, each row marked with the name of the resident. Here, indeed, there is a time to sow and a time to reap. During special growing seasons, we see cherry tomatoes and huge tomatoes, beans, lettuce, gigantic sun flowers and beautiful roses. What a treat! Of course, when the tomatoes ripen, others are invited to share the harvest.

Needless to say, we have a Garden Club for residents who like to share their knowledge. If you prefer growing a flower garden, you can do that as well. We learn what to plant as we spend more time in our new homes. There are certain plants that do well in a northern exposure, while others thrive in the east, west or south. Helen, the lady with the butterfly vine mentioned in another chapter, is growing the most gorgeous bougainvillea I have ever seen. She started with a small plant and has allowed it to grow against a wall and it hasn't stopped growing. We attribute it to her green thumb. Helen is a devoted gardener. In her own words, "I love the soil and outdoors. For me, it's a spiritual experience, which brings me close to God. We have so little control of nature. It's wonderful to plant a tiny seed...and see it grow...a garden is just a little bit of heaven."

As for indoor plants, we each have our favorites. Donna is an expert in orchids. Her home has beautiful specimens in many vibrant colors. She is a fountain of information when it comes to the care and nurture of orchids. I've been nursing a small struggling orchid that bloomed once and never again. I've consulted Donna and have been told to discard it, even though the leaves are thick and dark green and the many roots rising from the bottom look like monster tentacles. My mistake was that I cut off the stem of the blooming part. No one had ever told me not to do that. Oh, well.

In visiting the various apartments in our community, I marvel at the ingenuity and creativity of our residents. Each of us has a small ledge outside our front door. We can decorate our entrance on that ledge. Fresh flowers are one favorite decoration. You can almost discover the resident's personality by looking at the ledge carefully. Many of us change the ledge with the seasons and the holidays. We see bright flowers in the spring and summer, pumpkins in October, turkeys and pilgrims in November, and wreaths and Christmas decorations in December.

You don't need to give up what you love when you move to a well chosen retirement community. Not only can you continue enriching your life with your creative caring for plants, but you can also admire what your neighbors are doing with theirs.

Helen cited a small poem when we talked. It's a good way to end this chapter:

"A kiss of the sun for pardon;

The song of a bird for mirth;

One is nearer God's Heart in a garden

Than anywhere on earth!"

17

Pets: Special Companions

Many of us, regardless of age, yearn for a "significant other." At our age, we may have lost a husband or wife, but we still need companionship. This is when pets become very important to us. We may have had a pet when we were younger, for our children, for protection, or just for fun. Now this pet becomes the "significant other" in our lives. Few of us like to be alone. That's why we choose to live in a retirement community. That life becomes especially sweet when we have a pet.

I have a dog. His name is Ronnie. I found him nine years ago when my husband became ill and I thought he would enjoy the companionship of a dog. Little did I know that Ronnie would become my constant faithful companion while I cared for my husband and after he left me. I found Ronnie in a shelter. He was named Geronimo because he had lots of fuzzy hair.

When I finally had him groomed he was a full-fledged Schnauzer without papers. He was beautiful. We fell in love instantly. Naturally (all of us, pet-owners say this) he is very intelligent, faithful, and there for me whenever I need him.

This story will repeat itself when you meet other pet owners. People with cats will give you another version of instant love. A pet will do many things for you. Most important, it fills the need for feeling needed. Let's face it, our children, brothers or sisters, even grandchildren don't need us constantly. Of course they still might ask us to baby sit, but some hesitate to give us that responsibility. They think of us more as *their* responsibility and the need for *them* to take care of us. That's why they encourage us to live in the retirement community. A dog or cat really needs us. It trusts us. We give it daily nourishment, keep it clean, and we accept its undying love for us. We give it our love in return. It's a great partnership. We also get our daily exercise when we take our dogs on their walk, or play with our cats. And who needs an alarm clock? Our dogs, especially, help keep us on our healthy schedule.

Donna has a cat, Tigger. She describes her relationship with Tigger. "My husband died in April. The following December I moved into a retirement community; a wonderful community filled with wonderful people and multitudes of activities. My days were filled meeting new friends and learning new games and exercise routines. All was well until nightfall, and having lived my entire life with others in my home, my new apartment on the third floor made getting a dog somewhat impractical, so I decided on a cat. A fellow resident was a volunteer at a nearby animal shelter, a pet rescue organization, and she told me they had several wonderful cats needing a home. My family owned a black and white tabby cat when our children were young. She lived with us for 19 years. So my first thought was I would get another black and white cat to keep me company. The shelter had a beautiful black and white, long hair cat, but when I reached to pick him up, he hissed and I said, 'That is not my cat.' The commotion woke a small orange seven-month-old tabby that pawed at his cage. I asked to hold him and it was love at first sight. He nestled in my arms and kissed my cheek and I said 'That's my cat!!'

"His name is Tigger after the 'Winnie the Pooh' character because he has stripes on his tail. The name fits. He is so like Tigger in 'Winnie the Pooh,' lovable and full of energy. He loves to play with his mice and foam balls. He seldom leaves my side. He lies across my shoulders while I watch TV, lies on the desk when I am on the computer, and of course sleeps with me at night. I can't imagine life without Tigger. He is my friend for life."

There are many cats at our community, each loved by their own in a special way. Here is the story of Alice and Pushkit, the two cats owned by Margot.

"Momcat. That's the name my son sometimes calls me. It's also my e-mail address. Yes, I love cats...cats have always been my favorite animals. I like elephants, too, but they're not exactly house pets. My mother also loved cats, so I grew up with them. Mom had her own words for things. Cats were 'pushkits.' Sometimes she even called me her 'pushkit.'

"When I moved back to Houston from California to help take care of my triplet grandbabies, I soon adopted two kittens, brother and sister. Two, so they'd have each other to play with, since I would spend most of my time with the babies.

"Alice is named for a cat I had back in the seventies. She was white and gray and a real character. This Alice is a mostly white calico with black and brown spots, and is growing up to be quite a character, too. Pushkit is an orange and white tabby, named in honor of my mother.

"Pushkit and Alice moved with me to my retirement community, where they like looking at the world from their 4th floor windowsills. They like grooming each other, climbing on the high furniture, tops of doorways, their cat tower, and racing all around the apartment.

"Before I moved here I would pay someone to come

in and care for my kitties when I went on vacation. But now, we cat owners trade cat-sitting with each other, which is good for everyone.

"I love having my little furry friends to come home to, whether I am out for an hour or several days. Their antics make me laugh, and their purring affection gives me great joy."

Other pets at our community include a talking parrot, a great companion for his owner. Janette talks to her bird. She has also trained him to talk to other residents when they walk by her apartment. His original owner was a sailor and Janette had to clean up his language before he could become a "social asset."

Another chapter in this book deals with relationships. We have found that pet owners form a bond with each other, particularly dog owners. As we walk our pets, we meet and talk, or sometimes we go in opposite directions because some dogs like people better than other dogs. In any case, we know each other as Ronnie's mom or Rover's dad. After several such encounters we might find out the dog owner's first name, but we never forget Ronnie or Rover.

18

"Ninety" and Living Fully

Can seniors approaching age 90 and older be a real part of the unique generation we've been telling you about, seniors who are seeking a life of passion, risk and adventure? Let's take a look at the activities of this extended age group and see. We may be very surprised to see the tremendous vitality that they exhibit in an environment that supports them with challenging and rewarding endeavors.

"May Lucille join your table for dinner?" Why of course, all chime in and from that moment the conversation dials up a notch as Lucille energetically introduces some topic in which she has been involved. There is never a dull moment in the dinner hour when she is there to initiate or add commentary. But Lucille does more than just talk; she is an active participant in a number of the available activities in the community. She may even be seen in the exercise room in the directed exercise classes, with tai chi being one of her favorites. As reflected in her dinner table conversation, she is very much aware of the activities in the community, even those she doesn't participate in––adventure is in her very nature.

And then there is Tienna, whose penchant for decorative plants on her patio finds her at any change of weather doing just the right things to give beautiful life to those plants. Since her patio occupies a space just off one of the main hallways, many of us become energized just looking at the effects of her work in beautification, and even wish that we might be invited to join her for "a cup of tea." She also seems to be an unofficial leader of the "90s group," overseeing arrangements for a once a month dinner gathering.

Peg is involved in so many activities that it's hard to keep up with her. Her participation in the Bible study group is notable because she always comes well prepared to make important comments and, as well, to question things that she doesn't understand––this always contributes greatly to the general discussion. Today she has to leave the session a few minutes early in order to get to the meeting that the drama group is holding in the next hour, as they plan and practice for the next performance for the residents as a whole. Then there's the Book Club, which is an additional outlet for the pleasure reading she does regularly. She's also long been an active member of the choral group that practices weekly and performs for the community on special occasions. When talking with Peg, she sometimes expresses regrets about not having been able to travel the world, even though she has lived an active family life and occasionally makes trips to visit them in various areas around the U.S. You can see, Peg reflects an energetic approach to risk and adventure, and you would never guess that she is well into her "90s."

Lest you think that the "90s" include only women, a number of gentlemen less inclined to identify themselves as part of that age group may also be observed actively engaged in many activities. Sports, such as golf, billiards, and wii® bowling, or board games such as bridge and other card games are a frequent venue. Many are likely to be seen involved in bird watching, the Great Discussions group, or in the choral group mentioned earlier. Grant is even continuing to write poetry and hopes to publish yet another small volume. As mentioned elsewhere, he and his wife conduct a small poetry discussion group every week.

It soon becomes obvious that the energy to become active in new and engaging pursuits, though sometimes hampered by physical limitations, is very much present in our population of "90s" and older. The pursuit of adventure continues; passion, risk, and adventure may be less obvious to the outsider, but they still persist!

19

Not Fully Retired Yet

Does the thought of full retirement thrill you or dismay you? Or … are you somewhere in-between? For many of us it is or has been a difficult decision. One way to bridge the gap is to move into a retirement community while you are still working. A number of us here have done so. Among them are your authors. I've been here five years and still hold the title of "president" of a small publishing company. Granted, it is a part-time job, that gives me many opportunities to participate in social activities of the community. I have designated one of the bedrooms in my spacious apartment as my office and spend many hours at the computer fulfilling my obligations for the business. I have made this "office" comfortable, with a sofa (which also doubles as my dog's bed), bookcases, a desk, a computer, a printer and a fax machine, as well as the all-important telephone. I have even found a place for my old IBM electronic typewriter, where I like to type envelopes. It may not be the most modern office in the world, but it's just right for me. My dog likes it also.

Another good example is Jerry. Jerry is a successful CPA who moved into our community a few years ago and commuted daily to his job. One of his specialties is preparing income taxes. When some of us discovered this, we approached him to take on our tax returns as well. Now he has so many clients here that it is no longer necessary for him to commute to work. His work is right here.

Linda moved here while she held a position with an insurance company. Slowly she reduced the time she spent at the office until recently she decided that she was ready for full retirement.

Marty has been an inspector for elevators most of his life. He still works at it on a part-time basis. When I asked him why he chose to move here, he smiled and commented: "One day I was on a high ladder, leaning against a tall tree next to my house, trying to cut off a limb. I looked at the distance from the ground and asked myself, 'why do I need this?' Next thing I knew, Sandy and I decided to move to a safer environment."

Perhaps one of our most well-known residents is Vivien, a renowned author, who is frequently requested to present lectures in the United States and abroad. She has been active for the last five years while living in our community, and just recently has decided to retire completely.

Janice and Griff were both active in their careers when they moved here. Their motivation was very simple. They had witnessed severe medical hardships happen to some of their friends and had seen the havoc it caused for the families of these friends. That is when they decided they did not want those life-time decisions to be made by their families; they wanted to make the decisions themselves. If something were to happen to them in the future, they knew the staff at their retirement community would be first responders who would respect their well-planned decisions.

I have listed just a few cases of part-time retirement. In other words, if you are not ready to fully retire, don't let it stop you from selecting your perfect home of the future. Move in when you can take part in all of the advantages offered by a retirement community.

20

Traveling Here, There, and Everywhere

When my mother was 93 years old, she took her first airplane trip from the Midwest to California, and a few months later she flew to Texas and then back to Chicago. This was a remarkable achievement at her age, though when she was a young mother, she had migrated from Michigan to Wisconsin via train transportation with four young children in tow. I myself took my first airplane trip from Iowa to California when I was 24 and since then have flown to many places around the globe. Many of the super-seniors, about whom we have been talking in this book, have actually lived in countries other than the United States for periods of time, as petroleum engineers or in other professional capacities, or as family of those engineers. Thus, travel is a familiar theme among these super-seniors in their years of 70 and beyond, though the activity now may assume different dimensions.

For example, many of these seniors have accomplished much leisure travel since their retirement from the professional workforce. As a matter of fact, a number of these people have been enthusiastic members of Elderhostel®, now known as Road Scholars®. As you probably know, this activity puts one in direct contact with groups of others who are interested in a topic promoted in a particular area of the country and even in other countries. In this way they can study topics of interest that they share with others. At the same time the participants have the opportunity to travel and explore with others of like interest; thus, the name Road Scholars® emerged.

Since many of the residents have lived in other parts of the U.S., Texas is like a new territory, a state that has a rich collection of places to explore. At this residential community we have a transportation planner, part of whose job is to dream up exciting adventures to the state's treasures. A new adventure is planned for almost every week, with the travel taken via our own community bus. Sometimes the trips are overnight, with arrangements for lodging made at the destination of the particular treasure site. Occasionally a trip might be planned to a well-known gambling location in another state, a horseracing event, or even a dog race; these trips usually involve a several-night-stay. Since about 25 or so individuals might go on one of these trips, the trips present an ideal opportunity for residents' socialization and friendship development.

The community's vehicles also become available for individuals who decided to leave their automobiles behind when they moved. Thus, individuals, who no longer have their own transportation available, can travel to the grocery store or to nearby shopping centers via a bus and driver provided by the community. This process supports independence for our super-seniors as part of their living cost at the community. Individuals can also arrange to be driven to medical facilities and appointments for a cost to their insurance or to their monthly bill. They can even arrange transportation to and from the nearby airport when they wish to travel to other cities and states. Thus, many of us have had the pleasure of travel access without the burden of auto maintenance, as well as avoiding the stress of driving in a city marked by an abundance of moving vehicles.

For many of the super-seniors who are continuing to grow in mind and disposition, travel has become a great opportunity for growth as well as pleasure. Their newfound freedom from professional work and family responsibilities has opened wide expanses for them to experience the world. It seems that, barring health problems, seeing the world is a treasured activity. Some have even made it their goal to make sure that they have visited every state in the United States, and some have made it their goal to visit every country in the world. Sometimes they make these trips an opportunity to provide their children or grandchildren equal opportunities to see the world with them. Travel by ship seems to be especially sought. For example, a trip to Alaska or through the Panama Canal, or even a trip to continents such as Australia, New Zealand, or Africa, as well as Europe and Asia are on some seniors' travel lists.

One of the interesting things about such global wishes is that, when health no longer permits the actual travel, some of our super-seniors make arrangements for others in the community to enjoy video presentations of these far lands. This is especially gratifying to those who haven't had a chance to do the actual physical travel. For example, one couple has developed videotaped movies of several of their trips to countries in Central Europe. On these trips, they visited many historic religious sites and stopped to explore them. All of this is caught on their DVDs, which have become highly desirable "home" entertainment for community members sitting comfortably in their apartment living rooms.

Thus, travel here, there, and everywhere is definitely an integral part of the life of these super-seniors. They continue to believe that this is a special time of life for growth and enjoyment, whether through passive and vicarious participation in travel or in the active form.

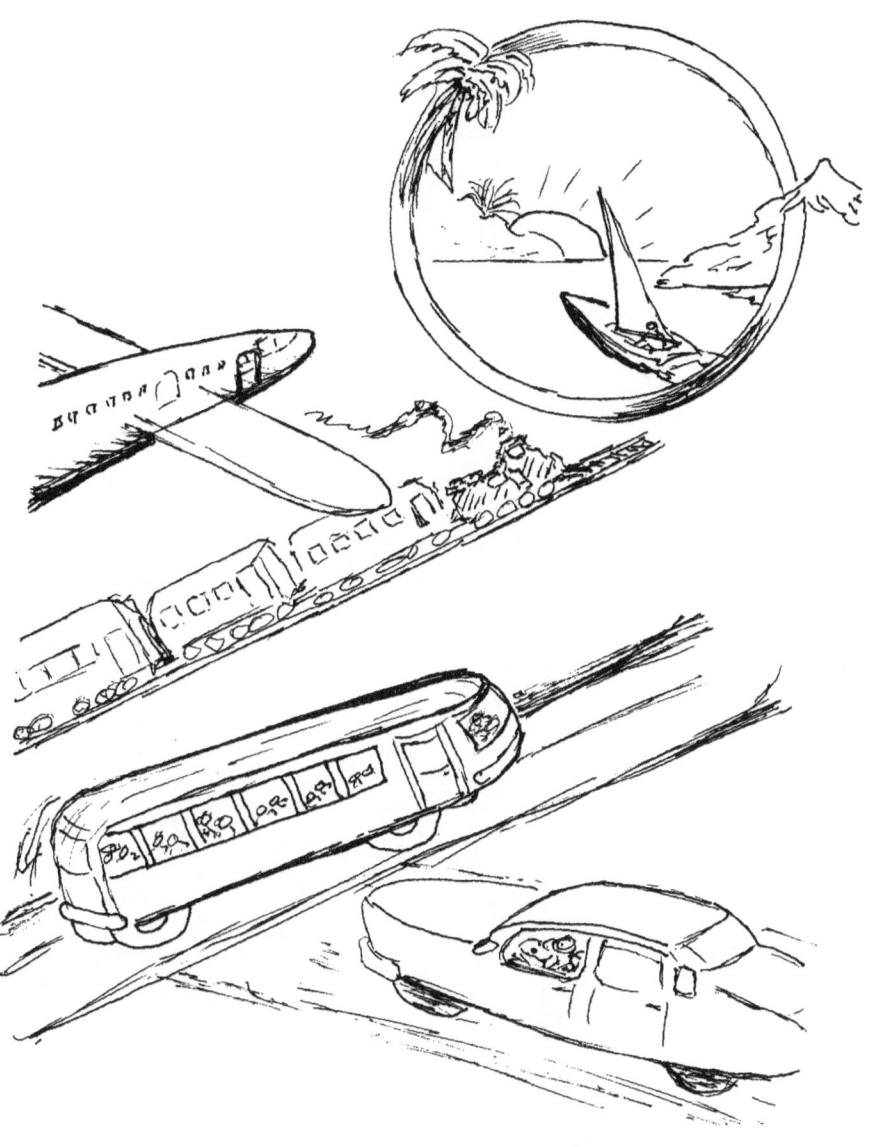

21

Technology – Tools and Challenges

Ah – technology! The greatest miracle of the 21st Century and the greatest challenge for us, super-seniors. Also a wonderful and exciting tool for our children and, especially, for our grandchildren, and the greatest source of frustration for us! Actually, it seems to cause a lot of frustration for our children at times too. I just spoke to my daughter, one of the baby boomers, in her fifties, and she was beside herself trying to work with her new oven. It seems she traded in her old one and had one of the newest electronic models installed in her kitchen. It consists of an oven and a microwave. She called the service number visible on the microwave and, after waiting 4 days for them to come, found out that her oven was made by a different company. She had to call them instead. Remember our ovens? We turned them on and we turned them off. Now every owner of one of these new models has to become a mechanical expert who has to choose among a dozen dials and knobs to find the answer to his or her cooking needs.

As far as the microwave is concerned, those came out when we were still in our prime. We figured them out and thank the inventors for making them available to us.

That brings us to computers. Have any of you felt a sense of embarrassment when your 5-year old grandchild sits in front of the computer and gleefully clicks out a power point presentation? How many of us actually know what a PowerPoint presentation is? Of course that's only the beginning. Daily we see new gadgets, I-phones, I-pods, smart phones (I thought only humans could be smart or dumb – they don't have a dumb phone), blackberries (I thought that was a fruit), and many, many more. I have asked my grandson several times to program my cell phone and how to use all the different options available to me. I can't help but think that life was a lot simpler when all these gadgets had not been invented.

The majority of us, super-seniors, don't want to be left behind in this "new world." Many of us attend computer classes, read books that have been "simplified" and plod ahead. We look at it this way: it keeps our brain active. It is said that "if you don't use it, you lose it." We certainly don't want to lose it.

I've talked to a number of our residents about this problem. The reaction is very mixed. Some refuse to have computers in their new homes, many have them but don't know how to use them, and yet a great number of us do like them. I love my computer but I haven't given up my typewriter entirely. I can't bear to give my old IBM Selectric away. As far as the cell phone is concerned, I believe the majority of us have adopted it. Not the complicated ones, but the simple ones where you can dial a phone number and receive calls. When I talk to my friends, they confide in me that their son, daughter, or grandchild has programmed it for them. That's a comfort. They also adjust it when it needs fixing. What really intrigues me is the "texting" feature on cell phones. I watch my grandsons texting messages to their friends without even looking at the keyboard. It reminds me of the time in my life when I learned to type. I guess texting is their answer. I don't think I'll ever learn it well enough to use successfully.

Some of us have other difficulties with the cell phone. I attended a theater performance with a friend, also a super-senior. In the middle of the first act, his cell phone sounded off. He tried and tried to turn it off, but he couldn't find the right button. He had to walk out of the theater to put the cell phone in his car so as not to disturb the rest of the audience.

Let's talk about television – a great entertainment

tool. Most of us wouldn't be without it. The improvements and new features continue to amaze me. Recently I bought a new television set with the flat screen. You can't see the buttons on it. If I should ever lose the control instrument, I would be lost. I know it's up there on the screen, but almost invisible. I still prefer the dials. It's interesting to see how the television set has grown, and I mean literally. The larger the screen, the more popular they are. I suppose that is called progress as well. Since most of us have moved from big homes into 1 or 2-bedroom apartments in our retirement communities, we still prefer the medium size screen. It fits our eyes better.

Many of us watch television regularly to find out what's going on in the world. That exposes us to the many advertisements interspersed in our favorite programs. The ads urge us to try new products and entice us with "specials for today only" and so on. I usually ignore them, but the other day I saw something that really interested me. It was an electronic gadget that emits a "supersonic" sound that only my dog can hear. If I ordered it right away, I would get 2 for the price of one. I was sold. My dog loves to bark when he sees another dog. He loves people, but with dogs it's a different story. This gadget would cure my dog from barking. Or so I thought. I ordered it and set one in the window where he loves to bark, and one in my office. Naturally I have no idea whether it works or not. It is only for my dog's ears. I didn't have to wait long. A dog walked in front of my window and Ronnie let out a huge howl, and another, and another. Perhaps my dog has a hearing problem, but I don't think so. So much for this electronic gadget. Now it's in the trash.

Don't get me wrong. I don't want to sound completely negative. There is a new electronic device that seems almost made for us, especially those of us with poorer eyesight. I am referring to electronic books. Although we still like the feel of a book with many pages in our hands, it is becoming more difficult to read small print. Yes, there are books available with large print but really an electronic book is ideal. We can adjust the size of the print for every volume and click a button when we have to turn a page forwards or backwards. It's a perfect size to carry in our purses when we expect a long wait at the doctor's or dentist's office.

Another positive side for technology is the continued progress being made in the medical field. Probably many of us wouldn't be around today if it weren't for the favorable results derived from medical technology and research. Hurrah for them!

I also don't want to imply that technology isn't helpful. Far from it. We love our battery-powered flashlights and handy telephones and of course the cell phones. I wonder what would happen if no more batteries were available? We really would be lost. But, since we are super-seniors, we do not have to worry about that. It won't happen in our life-time. We can enjoy the ease technology brings to our lives and let our children and grandchildren fix everything for us.

22

Selecting Your Ideal Community

OK, you have decided to consider moving into a retirement community for the rest of your life. Before you make a decision, you must consider a number of factors, because the goal should be happiness for you. Let's review some of the important ones:

1. finances - what can you afford
2. location – proximity to family and stores
3. residents and neighbors – will you feel comfortable with the folks
4. physical plan of the community – size and facilities
5. size of your apartment
6. food – probably one of the most important considerations
7. safety – medical facilities
8. staff – size and quality

9. pets – are you allowed to have any
10. privacy
11. entertainment
12. transportation

There may be other considerations important to you, but the ones listed here are important to everyone to some degree or another.

1) <u>Finances</u>

Can you afford to move to the community you like best? There are many plans available. Businessmen know that the numbers of super-seniors are growing, and there is an ever-increasing demand for good resident communities. Be sure to read the contracts carefully before you sign. Some require a certain amount of money down plus a monthly charge. This isn't necessarily a bad choice, especially if the contract states that the initial deposit will be returned to you if you move, or will go to your heirs after you are gone. The money might be available to you if you have a house to sell or some savings you are willing to invest without receiving a dividend. We found one community where the contract states that you are there for life, regardless of your financial obligations. That is worth considering.

Other communities may not require a down payment but will charge a higher monthly rental fee. It's up to you to make the choice. It might be a good idea to discuss the financial terms with your family, lawyer or financial adviser. The important thing is that you feel comfortable with your decision. Remember, you'll be spending the rest of your days in your chosen community.

2) Location

This is a very important consideration. When asked, many residents of retirement communities will tell you that they want to be near their family, or perhaps their family wants them close in case of future medical emergencies, or just because they worry about you. At our community, at least half of the residents are here because of this reason. They come from all parts of the country. They come because they want to be near their children and, particularly, their grandchildren. Some are here because their family chose the community for them.

This can be a problem. One resident, Dora, was quite unhappy because she was not consulted in the choice of retirement living. She liked her apartment but she would have liked to make her own choice. Be careful before you move. Be sure you have seen the place and will be happy to be there. It is difficult to move later, especially when you have reached the age where driving a car is no longer an option.

Other considerations when moving is the climate, the proximity to shopping, doctors, pharmacies, banking, visiting your loved ones, making new friends. You will have to leave some of these decisions to chance, but try to do your research before you move.

3) <u>Residents and neighbors</u>

Consider whether or not you will feel comfortable with the folks here. If you have a chance to visit your future home before you move, take a tour with the staff and then take a self-appointed tour, meeting residents and asking them questions important to you. You will get a feeling about the place and how you will fit in.

One good sign will be the friendliness exhibited by the current residents. What kind of person are you? Are you the type that never meets a stranger? Do you like to dress casually or do you like to be elegant? Do you like fancy meals or do you prefer cafeteria style? All these factors will become apparent to you when you shop for a retirement community. As we interviewed a number of our acquaintances who live here, we found out that the most important thing they were looking for was friendliness. For instance, at our restaurant the staff will seat you at different tables with different people. It does not matter whether you are single, a widower or widow, a married couple. You can be seated at a different table each evening or you can seek out a group of newly made friends and ask to be seated together. Mealtime is an excellent time for social gathering.

If, on the other hand, you wish to eat alone, you can

pick up your meal and take it back to your apartment. It is your choice.

4) <u>Physical plan of the community – size and facilities</u>

Do you want an intimate setting with perhaps 150 residents, or do you want to be part of a larger community of 500 or more? There are advantages and disadvantages to both. A small community will be homey and you will soon know everyone there. Naturally the staff will be limited as well as the amenities. I know a couple who recently moved into such a small community. They have a 2-bedroom cottage and walk to the main building for one meal a day. They have lots of privacy and that's how they like it. Their main inconvenience is walking to the main building when the weather is poor. They don't seem to mind that.

I live in a larger community. We have 500 residents and continue to grow. There are four buildings, all connected with interior hallways. We don't ever have to worry about the weather. There are two restaurants, one with table cloths and a sufficiently large staff, the other informal, cafeteria-style. We have our own bank, pharmacy, food market, and medical center. Each building is four stories high and all lead to the main building where we eat, play and conduct business.

What do you like? Shop around and choose. Our

group of super-seniors continues to grow and more communities become available every day.

5) <u>Size of your apartment</u>

This choice may not seem important right now but it should get your attention before you make your move. Most retirement community apartments consist of one or two bedrooms. That may come as a shock to those of you who live in spacious homes. You wonder how to decide what to take with you and what to leave behind. It will surprise you to find out that you can do with a lot less than you presently own. If you are moving from one apartment to another, the choice is not so difficult. Chances are you would not have to downsize at all.

At our retirement community there is a special staff member who is available to help prospective residents with the planning. It is also easy to construct or request a blueprint of the apartment under consideration. I enjoyed drawing furniture to scale and placing it different ways on the blueprint to see what fits where and to move it around until the rooms looked just right. If you have furniture for both a dining room and a kitchenette, you might want to decide between the two. I chose my kitchenette furniture because it had chairs on wheels that were easy to move, and table with a removable center leaf. How many closets does your apartment have? Do you have enough room to store your precious belongings?

Of course the most important consideration will be whether you are single or a couple. Needless to say, a couple will feel more comfortable with two bedrooms and two baths.

Another important concern is the location of your apartment. Do you want to be on the first floor, with perhaps a patio? This is especially convenient if you have a dog that needs to be taken for a walk several times a day. You might also prefer an apartment on an upper story where the view might be more inviting. How close do you need to be to the elevator?

All these factors need to be examined before you make your final choice. You'll discover many more.

6) <u>Food</u>

Many of the retirement communities will invite you (and your spouse) to a complimentary meal along with a tour of the facilities. Take advantage of this invitation. It is a wonderful way to find out what kind of food you will be getting. It is true that the meal might be a little more extravagant than the daily fare, but it won't be too far off. Be sure to ask the staff questions. How many entrees do they serve? How many vegetables? Salads? Soups? Desserts? How many meals are included in your monthly rent? During what hours are the meals served? How formal is the dining room? Is there an informal cafeteria-style restaurant on the premises? How about vegetarian dishes or other special requests?

Be sure you are happy with the quality of the food. Once you have moved in, it is too late to find out you don't like what is being served.

7) <u>Safety and Health</u>

Since moving into my retirement community, I've developed a regular pattern for the beginning of each day. My apartment is on the first floor and leads out to a small patio and garden. It's the perfect place for taking my small dog, Ronnie, for his morning walk. Ronnie is a Schnauzer, a sweet dog. He has one problem. He loves people but doesn't like other dogs. He barks at them and pulls on the leash to get to them. One particular morning Ronnie saw another dog approaching, pulled hard on the leash and succeeded in toppling me so that I lost my balance and fell over the metal edge of the flowerbed, and gashed my right leg. One of my neighbors saw what happened and called our emergency team. Within five minutes, two first-responders appeared with bandages, first aid equipment, etc. They quickly wrapped my wound, called an ambulance, and sent me on my way to the hospital. The neighbor took care of the dog.

This kind of response is a common occurrence at our community. Accidents can happen anywhere but the assurance that someone will take care of you immediately is one of the conveniences available at a good retirement community. We are fortunate to have a complete medical center with doctors, nurses and specialists. The specialists are available on an appointment basis. Just this month, September, an announcement was made that all of us could get our flu shots. We lined up and, voilá, it was done. No doctor appointments or visits to the local pharmacy. What a relief!

It's so nice to know that we are safe and well taken care of. In our apartments, each room has an emergency cord that, when pulled, brings an attendant to your door. Apartments are automatically equipped with specially designed baths, showers, and toilets that make their use safer. We are used to reading in newspapers and magazines that most accidents occur at home. These special safety devices in our homes work to keep accidents at their minimum.

Let's face it, at our age, we have become more fragile and need more care for our physical needs, even though we pride ourselves on our mental condition. When that starts to falter, there is someone here at all times to become aware of changes and do something about it.

8) Staff

In order for a retirement community to function efficiently, it must have a good staff. Be sure to have some contact with the employees before you decide where you want to live. For example, when you enter the main building, is the person seated at the information desk friendly, with a smile on his/her face, ready to help you?

At our residence we always look forward to mealtimes because we see bright young faces to seat us and serve us. These are high school students who participate in a scholarship program by serving as waiters and waitresses at our tables. They wear neat crisp uniforms, along with a name tag so that we can get to know them, and they seem happy to see us. What a treat! Most of them learn our names quickly and learn whether we like coffee or tea with our meal, or if we need anything special. It is hard to get this kind of service in a restaurant. We all know that. When these young people put in their hours, they not only get their salaries, but also the opportunity to receive a scholarship towards their college education. It's a win-win situation for everyone. Of course it also provides them with valuable practical experience.

The residence should provide you with an efficient staff that includes specialists in the various areas of maintenance and service. Be sure staff is available on a 24-hour basis. I remember recently calling the front desk at midnight because of a loud cricket sound that kept both me and my dog awake. Within five minutes a young man appeared with a ladder and a battery. From my description, the staff member had realized that my smoke alarm battery was losing power and fixed it accordingly. No sleepless nights for me or my dog.

9) <u>Pets</u>

We talked about pets in a previous chapter. Here we just want to emphasize the importance of checking at your new residence whether or not pets are allowed. For many of us the pet is part of our family and we certainly want that pet with us when we move.

What kinds of facilities are available for your dog, for example. Does he/she have a place to walk? Is there a place for you to dispose of his/her droppings? Does the residence reinforce cleanliness for the sake of all residents? These may appear as small matters, but you'll find that they are very important in a new residence. We must keep our dogs on the leash at all times when we walk with them. Be sure your residence enforces this rule. There is nothing more disturbing for some residents as having a dog running towards them or jumping on them. This may be important for you also.

A happy pet can mean the difference between loving your new home or feeling unhappy there.

10) <u>Privacy</u>

If you have always lived in a house, you will find apartment living quite different. You might also find it extremely pleasant. In both cases you have neighbors. You might have loved your neighbors or perhaps not. In a retirement community, privacy is respected. Even though the next apartment might only be a short distance away, we have found that people will not barge in on you. They will call ahead of time so as not to disturb you. This is an unwritten law that all of us honor. We also recognize that many of us would like to make friends and there is no problem there. A few weeks after moving in, we see groups forming as we meet each other, and find out what our preferences are. Another good place to meet is in the dining room, especially if the seating is not prearranged.

11) Entertainment

Most retirement communities have a social director or someone in charge of planning entertainment. If not, there will be some residents who will take on the job. At our place we have numerous clubs and activities to suit every taste. If one of the residents likes to play pool, he'll find others. Card games are too numerous to mention. Every morning you will find several tables playing bridge, canasta, Mexican train, and many others. Of course there is bingo for interested residents. Every month the social director plans trips, either one day, or longer. Just because we are super-seniors does not mean we don't like to have fun. Make sure your choice of retirement community includes opportunities for entertainment.

12) Transportation

For some of us, actually many of us, transportation becomes a problem when we reach the soaring seventies and beyond. Maybe we or our families have decided that it is no longer safe for us to drive. A good retirement community will have provided facilities for transportation, either daily scheduled trips to grocery and variety stores, or necessary trips to doctors and pharmacies. Find out what is available when you are looking. Quite often new neighbors will find help among other residents who still drive. That is a possibility, but you shouldn't count on it.

We may have overlooked some other questions, important to you. If so, don't hesitate to ask the staff or residents of the community you are considering. They'll be glad to help you.

23

Our Sense of Humor

What happens to our sense of humor when we become super-seniors? Different problems continue to face us involving finances, health, responsibilities, and whatever else we've carried with us throughout the 70+ years of our existence. No sense in worrying too much. There probably isn't too much we can do to change our situation. One thing we know though. We can laugh about it and share it with others who are in the same boat.

I took a trip to Austria a number of years ago and picked up a little souvenir that I still treasure and keep on the kitchen wall. It is a small frying pan with the following German inscription: "Humor ist wenn man trotzdem lacht!" (Humor is when you can laugh in spite of whatever happens!) We may see things differently at our age, but we can still laugh about them.

At the dinner table recently, we admired the young waiter who kneeled down beside each one of us to get our order. All of us thought that was admirable and, almost in one breath, we commented: "If any of us did this today, we'd never be able to get up again. Someone, younger than us, would have to pick us up off the floor." We burst out laughing. You might call this a sample of a super-senior's sense of humor.

Here is what happened to Betsy the other day. "Recently, while washing my hair, I heard a knock on my door. I considered ignoring the knock because my hair was wet and sudsy, but, when the knocking persisted, I knew it was important. I called, 'Who is it?' My neighbor answered, 'it's Kathy – I need your help.'

"I opened the door with soap running into my eyes and water dripping down my neck, to discover it was indeed an emergency. Kathy said, 'please, help me. A friend is coming to visit and I can't open this bottle of wine.' I immediately handled the emergency situation and saved the day for a dear friend."

Betsy decided that the inability to open a wine bottle must not be uncommon in a retirement community, because several weeks before the above incident she was passing an apartment and noticed a wine bottle opener, a bottle of wine, and a note on the shelf outside the door. The note read as follows: "Please open me!" She promptly complied with the request.

These incidents may not seem humorous to you if you have not reached the ripe age of 70+. For us, they are hilarious. It may be that we don't take ourselves too seriously anymore at our stage in life. We live with our shortcomings, find them humorous, and enjoy our existence.

Life is more fun when we can laugh at ourselves. Super-seniors have learned it well.

Epilogue:

Finding the Joys of 70 and Beyond

Our book began its focus on where and how to live the fourth quarter of our life in order that we might live it as fully and productively and happily as was meant for each of us. Now that we have traversed childhood, adolescence and the various stages of adulthood through developing work lives, family and friendship groups, and a multitude of creative endeavors, how might we most productively conduct our fourth quarter? Perhaps Betsy (one of our contributors) said it best in answer to the question of why she had engaged in her quest for this venue for her special fourth quarter. "To place myself in an environment with fewer responsibilities and less pressure, where I could relax and be at peace for the rest of my days." But listen to the rest of her response. "Yes! But much to my surprise, I found LIFE!!"

That is precisely what we have tried to convey in our discussions about the "ideal retirement community" and the special treasures and wealth of the "LIFE" that Betsy so joyously exclaimed she had found. Yes, we believe we have found life with a capital L in one special retirement community that we happen to call home. But we must keep in mind that life at any age does not come without price. In that regard we have tried to make sure that we were speaking forthrightly about the difficulties and hardships that might specifically accompany our age group. Thus, John in his letter talks directly about the loving care of a wife who has beginning dementia, but he also describes enthusiastically the many things she and he shared in their past life, while at the same time sensitively describing current care. He then goes on to describe the expanding, intellectually stimulating "LIFE" in which he is currently and enthusiastically involved.

Our philosophy about the activities described in our book is previewed well by Sara Lawrence-Lightfoot (*The Third Chapter. Passion, Risk, and Adventure in the 25 Years After 50)* who writes: "successful aging requires that people continue---across their lifetime---to express a curiosity about their changing world, an ability to adapt to shifts in their developmental and physical capacities, and an eagerness to engage new perspectives, skills, and appetites."

Lawrence-Lightfoot adds, "This requires the willingness to take risks, experience vulnerability and uncertainty, learn from experimentation and failure, seek guidance and counsel from younger generations, AND DEVELOP NEW RELATIONSHIPS OF SUPPORT AND INTIMACY" (caps added). That philosophy applies as well to the years of 70 and beyond as to the 'after 50' years, perhaps even more strongly and poignantly!

We have tried to convey those principles in the stories we chose to relate, and in the anecdotes and philosophy we have expressed about super- seniors soaring beyond 70, as told in this book, *A Unique Generation:70+ Living "it up" in a Retirement Community*. We hope that our tales will have helped you determine how and where you too might soar and more fully find LIFE!